BOTTLE GARDENING

BOTTLE GARDENING

Peter McHoy

LINE DRAWINGS BY VANESSA LUFF
PHOTOGRAPHS BY PETER MCHOY

BLANDFORD PRESS
POOLE · DORSET

716
Mchbgar 99

First published in the UK 1985 by Blandford Press,
Link House, West Street, Poole, Dorset, BH15 1LL

Copyright © 1985 Peter McHoy

Distributed in the United States by
Sterling Publishing Co., Inc.,
2 Park Avenue, New York, N.Y. 10016

British Library Cataloguing in Publication Data

McHoy, Peter
   Bottle gardening.
   1. Glass gardens
   I. Title
   635.9′85   SB417

ISBN 0 7137 1464 6 (hardback)
ISBN 0 7137 1584 7 (paperback)

Technical advice, cutting and all equipment
for cover photograph were very kindly provided
by Doctor Peter Thompson, "The Garden School",
Norton St. Phillip.

Typeset by Graphicraft Typesetters Ltd, Hong Kong
Printed by Biddles Ltd Guildford, Surrey, U.K.

CONTENTS

c|

INTRODUCTION

Not long ago, bottle gardening was a rather esoteric branch of gardening followed by comparatively few. In recent years more and more people, gardeners and non-gardeners alike, have begun to appreciate what a fascinating hobby it can be.

Throughout this book the term 'bottle' has been used loosely. 'Terrarium' has been taken to mean a container other than a bottle; but to save repetition 'bottle' has been used for advice that applies to all containers, whatever their shape.

Most of the planted bottle gardens sold in shops are pretty, but they bear little resemblance to traditional bottle gardens. There is nothing wrong in this; the open-topped commercially-produced bottle gardens are just another way of displaying plants attractively, but the open bottle greatly increases the type of plants that can be grown, and many of the bottle gardens suggested in this book are of that type. The true bottle garden, however, is more than a display case; it is a sealed environment in which plants can grow undisturbed for months, even years, without attention.

1. HOW BOTTLE GARDENING STARTED

The bottle garden had a very practical beginning. The principle of a sealed environment was developed with the intention not of *displaying* plants but simply of keeping them alive. Bottles were not used, but hefty glass cases that resembled miniature greenhouses.

The origin of the modern bottle garden lies in the smoggy atmosphere of London in the 1830s. Dr Nathaniel Bagshaw Ward, an amateur botanist, nursed an ambition to grow ferns in the back yard of his house in the dockland area of London, but they simply would not thrive in the polluted atmosphere, and at one stage he gave up the idea. Success came unexpectedly and indirectly, while he was studying how a sphinx moth emerged from its chrysalis (not an easy task as the caterpillar normally burrows underground for this stage of its life cycle). Dr Ward's solution was to bury the chrysalis in moist earth in a bottle, which he closed with a lid; an action, coupled with observation, that was to have a profound effect on the successful transportation and introduction of many exotic plants, and eventually to lead to a fascinating hobby now followed by many thousands.

His interest in the sphinx moth was soon replaced by other things that began to happen within the bottle. He noticed that during the warm part of the day moisture vapour was given off by the soil and formed condensation inside the glass, only to run down the sides of the bottle and back to the earth. Moisture was going through a regular cycle. This in itself was interesting, but before the moth emerged something more exciting happened. A grass had begun to grow, and so had a fern — one that he had tried unsuccessfully to grow before. Here it was growing and thriving without care.

He deduced that ferns needed the sort of conditions found in the bottle: humidity and constant moisture, still air, and freedom

7

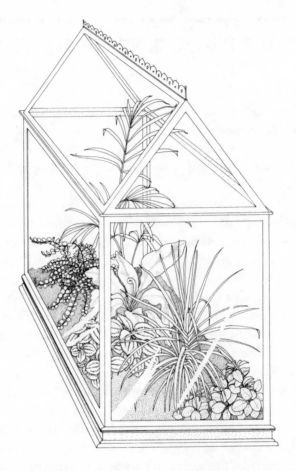

An example of a Wardian case. These are now used purely for decorative purposes.

from pollution. He let the fern grow on, and it flourished in the bottle for nearly four years, *without water being added or the top removed*. It is due largely to that plant (a form of male fern, *Lastrea filix-mas*, now included in *Dryopteris filix-mas*) that we can trace the origins of bottle gardens.

Dr Ward was stimulated to experiment with other bottles and glass cases, trying different plants. One of his most spectacular successes was with the Killarny fern (*Trichomanes speciosum*), a notoriously difficult plant to grow, thriving in nature near waterfalls and damp caves where the atmosphere is constantly moist; in normal cultivation the thin, very delicate, foliage almost always dries out. He succeeded in growing one of these plants in a bottle for four years until it became too big and had to be transferred to a fern house where it was covered with a bell jar.

The bottles were replaced by more elaborate glazed cases, and these became quite fashionable as drawing-room features as well as serving a more scientific purpose. Wardian cases, as they had become known, solved the problem of transporting new plants back during the long sea voyages from distant lands. Many of the plants collected by explorers usually died during the many months the sea crossings took, with extremes of temperature and salt spray as added hazards. Wardian cases helped to protect the plants from the sea air and drying winds, and the good growing conditions within the cases greatly improved the quality and quantity of new living plants being sent back.

Ward was acclaimed by scientists and public alike, and he exhibited a bottle at the Great Exhibition in the Crystal Palace, London, in 1851. It contained ferns and mosses that were in perfect health and had not received fresh water for eighteen years. In the second edition of his book *On the Growth of Plants in Closely Glazed Cases*, he said he believed that it would be possible 'to fill a case with palms and ferns (placing it in a position where it would always have sufficient light) and that it would not require water for fifty or a hundred years'.

Do not let that optimism lull you into wishful thinking. A bottle garden will need fairly regular attention (at least every couple of months) unless you have just the right balance and the right plants, and even a bottle of small ferns and mosses will benefit from an annual once-over.

Nevertheless, Dr Ward showed the way to a fascinating facet of gardening that *anyone* can enjoy whether or not they have a garden, one that needs the minimum of effort and skill provided that you get things right in the first place . . . and one where you can enjoy your plants the year round whatever the season.

2. MODERN BOTTLE GARDENS

Few ready-made bottle gardens on sale in shops and garden centres are sealed bottles. Most of them are open-topped, and many of the plants used are too vigorous for a sealed bottle that would be expected to last for many months without attention.

Nowadays, shop-bought bottle gardens are likely to be plant arrangements in which the bottle is merely treated as an attractive and convenient holder. As short-term arrangements, they are perfectly satisfactory; and once the plants outgrow the bottle you can take them out and start again, this time making a sealed bottle if you prefer.

SEALED OR OPEN?

There is little point in being dogmatic about which is best. Both sealed and open bottle gardens have their advantages, and their limitations. To dismiss either is to narrow the possibilities enormously.

A sealed bottle can last for years without attention, *if the bottle is properly balanced* (see p. 44) *to start with, and provided you select suitable plants*. If moss-like plants and ferns do not appeal, and you prefer something bolder and perhaps even in flower, you will find a sealed bottle frustrating and troublesome, if not dull. On the other hand, ferns and mosses can make charming bottle plants, and there are other foliage plants that can be included successfully in a sealed bottle if you are prepared to accept form and shape rather than colour.

Many of the plants in bought open bottles are attractively coloured or variegated, and by looking through the open top of a coloured bottle you can appreciate them more easily. In a sealed carboy, however, everything is likely to be seen through dark green glass; so bear in mind that what might seem an attractive foliage plant will look far more muted when planted, although the variegation will still be seen.

Quite apart from the obvious effect of looking at everything through green glass, the poor light will also affect the variegation on many plants. Small plants of variegated euonymus are often used in bottles, but the bright cream and green variegation will rapidly turn to a much less striking light and dark green in poor light. You can buy transparent bottles, but these are much less widely available.

Any plant in a sealed bottle must be able to tolerate constantly damp, humid conditions and poor light. If you add to this the fact that they should not be too vigorous, then the range of plants that will be really successful is much more limited than for an open bottle.

The advantages of a sealed bottle can be sheer charm (the greens and the interesting shapes of plants such as ferns and selaginellas can be extremely effective), and ease of maintenance. Once the bottle is established there is nothing to do except enjoy it for months, perhaps even a year, at a time. Holidays are no

A modern bottle garden.

problem, and even if you are not normally 'green fingered' with house plants, within reason you can neglect a sealed bottle and still be confident of success.

An open bottle will enable you to grow a much wider range of plants, introducing more colour and variety (possibly even flowers if you are willing to take the extra care necessary). Because you can see into the bottle through the top the colours can be appreciated better; and many plants will benefit from the extra light (though they may be drawn towards it so that you soon have a bunch of elongated stems appearing in the neck).

Although moisture will be lost through the open neck, you will still need to water the plants far less frequently than you would if they were in pots. Once a month may be sufficient for most of the year, perhaps once a week in the hottest months. So they are still an easy way to grow many small houseplants.

The difficulty is keeping the compost sufficiently moist without

An example of what can go wrong if you choose an unsuitable plant. This hypoestes has become drawn and leggy.

being waterlogged. You will have to water regularly, and each time you run the risk of overwatering. Because there are no drainage holes, the compost can soon become waterlogged and the plants will then rapidly deteriorate and die.

CASES AND DOMES

Apart from the traditional carboy, there are many other suitable containers, from antique bell jars or glass domes to sweet jars and wine bottles or goldfish bowls (see p. 17). Many of these are made of clear glass, which enables you to appreciate the colour of the plants better, and means that growth should be sturdier; you must, however, be more cautious where you place them. Although good light is desirable, strong sunlight through the window and then clear glass could scorch the plants.

In Chapter 3, there are many examples of containers that can be used to display your plants, and they all have a place. The only constraint is to bear in mind the size and shape of the plants, and whether or not they are suitable for a stoppered container.

TERRARIUMS

'Terrarium' is a term loosely used to describe a plant case, an aquarium being the most obvious easily-adapted candidate. You can buy elaborate modern imitations of the old Victorian plant cases (see p. 19), but these are expensive and not necessarily any better than an aquarium for the plants. As many aquariums are easily fitted with a light they also have a distinct advantage when it comes to healthy plant growth.

A fluorescent tube of the type sold for aquariums should give light of the right kind for plant growth. Ordinary fluorescent tubes have light of the wrong wavelength for good plant growth, and filament lamps could generate too much heat.

A terrarium will give you much more scope for miniature 'landscaping' than a bottle, as rocks, even tiny pools, can be introduced.

13

3. FINDING THE RIGHT CONTAINER

Suitable containers can be expensive. At 1984 prices you could pay more than £20 for an empty carboy, and a modest aquarium could cost you as much. If you want to buy a 'leaded light' terrarium or plant case of reasonable size then you could easily pay over £50. It pays to shop around, however, as you might be able to find a *planted* bottle that costs less than the empty container. It may also be possible to pick up a second-hand aquarium quite cheaply. It does not even matter if it leaks (you should be able to seal it adequately for a garden). Jumble and junk sales may reveal the most surprising bargains, so bottle gardening does not have to be an expensive hobby. Just keep your eyes open; an imaginative eye will see possibilities in all kinds of containers.

TYPES OF CONTAINER

The ideas presented here for types of container are by no means exhaustive, but they should indicate some idea of the potential, and stimulate the imagination.

Carboys

Everyone's idea of a bottle garden container. The genuine acid carboys used for chemicals are seldom used nowadays. Most of the green bottles that you see are made as decorative containers. The green ones are mainly made in Spain (where they are used for pickled olives), but there are some transparent bottles (in a wider range of shapes) imported from Italy.

Choose the largest size that you can afford: a small one of 18cm (7in) diameter is really too small to be effective. The surface area of glass to growing space tends to make the bottle look more

A carboy makes an extremely attractive container.

glass than plants, and you will have space for only a few small plants. A diameter of 30-38cm (12-15in) will look better proportioned and provide a lot more scope for planting. Although a squat shape can look particularly attractive, a more upright outline is better if you want to grow upright plants.

A purpose-made carboy/bottle can be expensive. Compare the price with an equivalent planted garden; it may be no more expensive to buy one with the plants in (you can always remove unsuitable plants, to use as pot plants, and replace with more suitable ones).

Aquariums

There is no point in buying an expensive aquarium for your plants. You should be able to buy a second-hand one quite cheaply at a jumble sale or from card advertisements in shops.

Some aquarium shops sell new ones cheaply if they are damaged, which probably will not matter for your display (see Plate 8).

Do not worry if it is not watertight. Even if you want a miniature pool it should be possible to arrange this in a separate small container, and in any case small leaks can be blocked with an aquarium sealant.

You are unlikely to be able to treat the aquarium (which you can now call a terrarium) as a sealed environment, but you can reduce the moisture loss by placing a well-fitting sheet of glass over the top. Most modern aquariums have a ledge a couple of centimetres from the top to support a sheet of glass. As you will want yours to be close-fitting (take the exact measurements to a glass merchant, who should be willing to cut the glass to size), you will need some means of lifting the glass out. A simple but effective method is to fix a couple of large marbles (one at each end) to the glass with a glass adhesive, available from most hardware shops. These should be adequate to lift the glass enough to get your fingers beneath it.

Whether or not you use a glass top, an aquarium light will greatly enhance the display, and improve plant growth. You should be able to buy an aquarium top that will take a fluorescent tube. Make sure you buy a tube from an aquarium shop (or ask for one suitable for plant growth if you buy elsewhere) as an ordinary tube will not be suitably balanced for plants.

Because the glass over an aquarium will be horizontal, drips can be a problem. In a normal bottle garden they run down instead of falling on the plants. You may find it necessary to wipe the glass once a day, or turn it over, in which case you may need to fix marbles on both sides.

Specimen jars

Jars of the type used to preserve biological specimens can be more attractive than an aquarium, although the general advice is the same. A laboratory equipment supplier may be able to provide them.

Goldfish bowls

These offer only limited scope, because you will not be able to seal them and the open top is large in relation to the area of compost, so little moisture is conserved. Most are also small and you should not expect to accommodate more than one plant. This can, however, be effective if you choose a flowering plant of the right compact habit, such as an African violet (saintpaulia), or a carpeting plant that can eventually grow up the sides and out over the rim. *Soleirolia soleirolerii* (syn. *Helxine soleirolerii*) can be extremely effective, especially in the golden form, as can the miniature *Fittonia verschaffeltii* 'Argyroneura Nana'.

Overwatering can be a problem with a goldfish bowl. Regular watering will be necessary, yet the lack of drainage calls for careful judgement.

A goldfish bowl with the right plant can look very attractive.

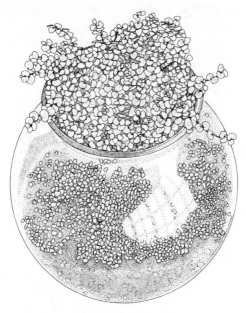

Domes

Domes are extremely attractive, especially if you are lucky enough to find a Victorian glass dome or bell jar. These are ideal for the plants, and make an interesting display. If you are not fortunate enough to have an old-fashioned glass dome you can buy the modern equivalents; unfortunately they have drawbacks.

Plastic domes are inexpensive, and probably worth buying to experiment with even if they fall far short of the real thing. It is likely to have a small hole in the top, which means that you will not have a sealed environment, although you will not have to water often because most of the moisture will condense and run back. Unfortunately, condensation on plastic is much more troublesome than on glass; it tends to cling rather than run down freely. Even though the dome is not sealed, condensation will still be a problem at times.

Plastic has another shortcoming: it is easily scratched and marked. Even small scuffs and scratches can be distracting as the light catches them.

Shallow glass domes, like the one illustrated in Plate 4, look appealing, but they are expensive (expect to pay more for the

A plant dome.

dome and base than for a planted carboy), and are not very practical. There is so little height that you are severely restricted with the plants that you can use, and there is even less room towards the edges! There is also very little depth in the base for compost, which again restricts the size and type of plant. These are best treated as a display for one flowering plant such as a saintpaulia (African violet), or for a moss or selaginella garden.

Domes are perfectly suitable for flowering plants, as they are so easy to lift off to remove the dead flowers. Even so, it is best to select a long-lasting plant that is not constantly dropping dead petals; a fibrous-rooted begonia, for instance, would be a constant problem because although there is a succession of flowers there is also a constant succession of dead flowers to decay.

Glass cases

The old Victorian plant cases are collectors' pieces now, and anyway too heavy and bulky for many modern homes. There are plenty of modern versions available, and although these are very appealing they need to be thought about carefully before you buy them. Many are more decorative than practical.

First decide whether you want a sealed garden, as many of them have one pane missing, which may be just what you want to allow your ivy to grow out through the side or top — but this makes a sealed unit impossible. Others have small hinged panes that allow access, and these should create a suitable environment even if they do not make a good seal.

The other drawback to some of these modern purpose-made terrariums is the small size of many of them. Although cost may encourage you to opt for a small one, you will find little scope for planting in many of them. They can still be effective, however, if you keep to very small plants such as mosses, or have just one larger plant, such as a fern or a small-leaved ivy.

The Tiffany process, using sheet glass to form the geometric designs, is still used, the panes being bonded with copper foil which is then soldered to the desired shape. You can make one of these yourself, but if you do it is best to start with a kit (see pp. 21-3).

Acrylic plastic is sometimes used, and this offers the opportunity for alternative shapes, but these lack some of the 'old fashioned' appeal.

Sweet jars

Most sweet jars are plastic now, but a few firms still use glass. If you ask at your sweet shop you may be able to buy a jar, the shop will almost certainly make a small charge to cover the deposit that they have to pay on the jars, but you will have a very inexpensive bottle garden.

Sweet jars have the merit of clear glass, which means that you can see the plants, and particularly colours, more easily. The biggest drawback is the limited headroom for the plant. You could stand the bottle upright for tall plants, but the limited planting space will restrict the planting possibilities.

If you keep to low-growing plants, such as *Fittonia verschaffeltii* 'Argyroneura Nana', mosses and dwarf selaginellas (some will be too tall), you will have a charming bottle garden at little cost. This is an ideal project for children.

A sweet jar is especially suitable for children learning to look after a bottle garden.

MAKE YOUR OWN TERRARIUM

There are some delightful terrariums in the shops — you can have your own 'antique' plant case without the need to hunt for the genuine thing. If you feel that you are unable to afford one, or simply fancy the challenge of making one yourself, it is possible to buy a do-it-yourself kit. It could even start you off on a new hobby.

Making one from a kit is a comparatively inexpensive way of acquiring a 'leaded' terrarium, but you will need a heavy-duty soldering iron (75 watt); if you do not already have one it could add almost half as much again to the cost. Of course, the soldering iron is a once-only cost, and you may find it useful for other jobs even if you do not make another terrarium.

All the glass will be cut for you already, and the kit should contain all the materials needed, including copper foil, flux, copper sulphate, brushes for the chemicals, and solder (1). What you do need is patience if you have not done anything similar before; it is likely to take you a day to finish, and you may begin to appreciate why they are quite expensive to buy. On the other hand, there is a real sense of satisfaction at the end of it.

What is involved

The first job is to edge each piece of glass with copper foil (2). This comes in a strip the right width to fold over the sides when you place the glass in the centre. Although a bit tricky if you do not have nimble fingers, the knack is soon acquired. The strip is sticky and clings to the glass; the edges are simply rubbed smooth with a pencil.

The tricky part is joining the pieces of the jigsaw. You can try to support the upright and angled pieces with blocks of wood while you tack solder them in place at the corners. One extra pair of hands will be better than a dozen pieces of wood.

The various parts are fluxed and soldered on the inside as each layer of the terrarium is built up (3). If you have not soldered before you may find it difficult to get an even line of solder to

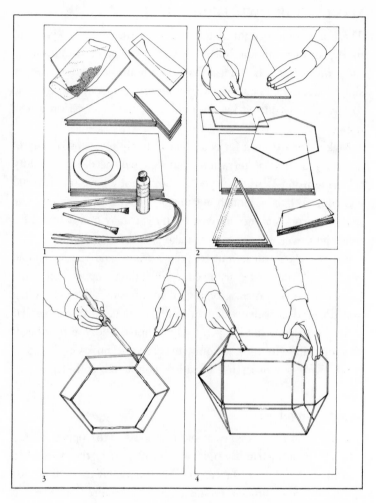

start with, but fortunately the section that you begin with will be the bottom and covered by compost, and you will almost certainly quickly improve enough to solder decent joints for the rest of the terrarium.

The top is the most difficult part to assemble on your own. A block of wood of exactly the right dimensions can be used to support the apex while the pieces are tack soldered; but again an extra pair of hands will prove invaluable.

If your alignment is less than perfect, do not worry. The solder

Terrariums increase the type of plants that you can use.

covers up all kinds of gaps, and the chances are that you will find the finished job perfectly acceptable.

By the time you turn your attention to soldering the outside of the joints, you will probably have gained enough experience and confidence to make a neat finish.

As a final touch, the solder is brushed with a copper sulphate solution to give it a duller, less shiny finish (4).

Kitchen jars

These are inexpensive, and you should be able to buy one with a close-fitting glass lid. Although too small for an arrangement, they can be used for an individual plant, and look just right in the kitchen with herbs. You could, of course, grow the herbs in pots without glass protection, but grown in glass jars on the kitchen windowledge they make a good talking point, and you can take *fresh* herbs from a jar. Herbs should always be grown in a wide-necked jar to make it easy to snip off a few leaves when needed.

Chives grown in a kitchen jar.

Giant brandy snifters

These can be used for a plant display, but as the top is very open these must be regarded as little more than a decorative way of displaying plants in an open container. They look attractive but you have neither the benefit of an enclosed atmosphere nor the ease of managing plants with adequate drainage. Watering needs considerable care: the compost must dry out enough to remain aerated, but not be so dry that the plant is stressed by lack of moisture.

The open top and cautious watering means that you will not be able to use many of the plants that thrive in a proper bottle garden. Some succulents could be effective if you want a small arrangement of plants, but a single flowering plant can look particularly impressive; perhaps a *Kalanchoe blossfeldiana* or a saintpaulia (African violet).

An advantage of this type of container is the easy access to the plants, which will make it simple to remove faded flowers.

Food jars

These are not promising objects, but children can use them for bottle garden experiments. They could try germinating fern spores and watch the interesting life cycle — from spore to prothallus and gametophyte and then young sporophyte, the stage that we readily recognise as a fern. When the ferns become too large they can be discarded or promoted to one of your bottle gardens.

Mosses also provide possibilities: one moss type to each jar.

The different types can be studied at close quarters and their growth and eventual 'flowering' studied.

A jar with a screw top is the most convenient as it is so simple to use. If the top is one that you have pierced or punctured, however, try a small piece of cling film over the top, or even a jam-jar cover. This does not look particularly elegant, but no shade is cast.

Wine bottles

These can be tried if you want a real party-piece. The narrow neck creates a real 'ship in a bottle' dimension. The choice of

Wine bottles have their limitations, but can provide a most interesting feature.

plants is severely limited; very small-leaved creeping species are the practical solution. *Fittonia verschaffeltii* 'Argyroneura Nana' works (the 'Nana' part of the name, which means 'dwarf', is crucial; the large-leaved kind would be far too big). The creeping fig (*Ficus pumila*) also works.

A collection of bottles suitable for use as bottle gardens.

WHERE TO BUY

Jumble sales and junk shops are often rich grounds to search. There is always the danger that your own home will end up resembling a junk shop, but you can always discard anything that does not work. Be prepared to experiment, but willing to face reality if something does not really pay off.

Antique shops can yield some super containers, from antique Wardian cases and Victorian glass domes to less conventional glass containers that may appear to have little practical use — except perhaps to display plants in.

The drawback of antique shops is that you have to pay for the fact that they have to make a living.

Green or transparent glass carboys can sometimes be bought from garden centres, but they are more likely to stock ready-planted bottles. If the price is right, or if you have difficulty obtaining a suitable bottle, you may be prepared to remove any unsuitable plants to grow on as pot plants, and start again with the carboy.

4. POSITIONING

If a bottle garden or terrarium is to be appreciated, it must be seen. Unfortunately the best position for the plants is not always the most decorative position in the room. Striking the right balance is the key to getting the best from your bottle or terrarium.

Green carboys are a particular problem, as coloured glass filters out much of the light necessary for healthy growth. The amount of light inside the container can be as little as half of that outside, and more importantly the green colour acts as a filter for the wavelengths that are particularly useful to plants.

A windowledge that does not receive direct summer sunshine is the best place for a coloured carboy in terms of light, but unless you are fortunate enough to have a very broad windowledge space is likely to be a problem. Many carboys are large, broad as well as tall, and look precarious perched on a narrow ledge. There is also a risk that a sealed carboy may overheat in a sunny window during the summer. A table beneath the window is ideal; it is that much further from the window to reduce the risk of overheating during a hot summer. The light will still be fairly good, the bottle will not look precarious, and on the right sort of table will make an interesting room feature.

If you want to move a carboy or terrarium further into the room, try to move it to a lighter position from time to time. With a heavy bottle it is not always easy, but if you have two bottles you could alternate them weekly — one within the room, one near a window.

If you are unable to provide good light, choose your plants carefully. Ferns and green-leaved foliage plants are more likely to succeed than variegated foliage plants. Do not try to grow flowering plants in poor light unless you are willing to treat them as expendable. A flowering plant in a goldfish bowl or brandy

Ideal positioning for the various types of bottle garden within the living room.

snifter may look perfectly well for a couple of weeks even in quite poor light, by which time it will almost certainly have started to deteriorate, when you can discard the plant (it may not have cost any more than cut flowers for a couple of weeks), and start again.

You can buy terrariums designed to fit in a corner (triangular in outline). Be very cautious with these. They look attractive, but corners are usually dark places. Even corners near a window may be darker than a position within the room, unless the windows go very close to the side wall, and there are no heavy curtains drawn to the side.

Terrariums normally have clear glass, so there is more light for the plants, but they still need similar treatment to a green carboy. However, the better level of light in the container should enable you to grow a wider range of plants.

Because the plants used in bottles and terrariums are usually small, they need to be as close to eye level as possible to be appreciated. That is why they are almost always more effective on a table or on a ledge. Even a low table can make a significant difference, and of course if it is near the window the bottle will be that much nearer the light.

An aquarium or other kind of terrarium with a light provides much more scope. You must, however, be prepared to *use* the light, and even if it is in a room that you do not use every day get into the habit of switching on the light regularly. An aquarium will be fitted with a fluorescent tube, and these are a good choice for other terrariums, as they generate good light with little heat (you do not want to grill the plants). Always use a tube balanced for good plant growth, with high levels of light at red and blue wavelengths); you are more likely to find these stocked by an aquarium supplier than an electrical shop. Another reason for going to an aquarium shop is that any fittings they sell are likely to be safe in a humid atmosphere. Do not use ordinary fluorescent tube holders in a terrarium. On days when the light is poor anyway, you could leave the lights on all day; otherwise turn them on for the evening, say from tea-time until you go to bed. If you do this as a routine the plants should receive enough supplementary light to keep them growing.

Suitable narrow-necked bottles can be made into table lamps by buying a suitable fitting from an electrical shop. These are inexpensive and perfectly adequate for a sealed bottle. You will need a fitting that has a section to press into the top of the bottle (this may have plastic 'fins' that can be trimmed or compressed for a good fit) with the flex coming out of the side (with ordinary fittings that flex comes out of the bottom, which would not be suitable). These should be safe electrically if you seal the top adequately. You can use an ordinary light bulb, but you can buy special bulbs that will produce light more suitably balanced for plant growth. You are more likely to find these bulbs at a garden centre than a normal electrical shop. These are much more expensive than ordinary bulbs, but better for the plants. Always choose a wattage within the safety limits of the shade (this should be marked on the shade when you buy it, otherwise ask). As table lamps are usually placed where light is most needed — in dark areas or corners — either keep the lamp in a light place until you need to use it, or turn it on *regularly* as described for terrariums. The cost of running these lamps is not great, and they will enhance the room by making more of a feature of your indoor garden.

A bottle garden can be very effective in a bedroom, where many people tend to avoid keeping pot plants. Many pot plants do very well in bedrooms, and are most unlikely to do you any harm, but if you are anxious about this sort of thing then a bottle garden should be an attractive feature that you can enjoy without concern. In its own sealed environment it will grow happily, and can look good on a dressing table near a window.

Bottle gardens frequently end up on the floor for lack of anywhere more suitable to stand them. There are two ways of solving the problem that will also make them more of a feature. A *small* bottle can be suspended in a macramé hanger, or you could buy a bottle stand (see p. 32). If you use a hanger, you must bear in mind the weight of the bottle and compost, and ensure that it is suspended from a hook properly secured to a beam. Try

An attractive bottle garden stand.

to suspend the bottle so that it is quite low; even near a window the amount of light received will fall off dramatically if it is too high. If you buy a stand, always measure your bottle first to make sure that it will fit.

1 (top left) A sealed bottle containing *Asplenium nidus* (centre), and (clockwise from the small-leaved variegated ivy) *Peperomia clusiifolia* 'Jeli', adiantum, *Euonymus japonicus* 'Microphyllus', *Selaginella krausiana* 'Aurea', and *Cryptanthus acaulis*.

2 (below left) A collection of pileas. Clockwise from the back they are *P. cadierei, P. spruceana,* and *P. involucrata*.

3 (top right) This bottle has a *Dracaena marginata* 'Tricolor' as its central feature.

4 (below right) If the bottle has a wide neck the plants are more easily viewed from above. In this bottle *D. marginata* 'Tricolor' is surrounded by selaginellas and a small-leaved ivy.

5 A dome tends to be most effective with a simple display, with one dominant plant, such as this kalanchoe.

6 A bottle garden lamp is an interesting variation on the general theme. The main plant here is *Codiaeum* 'Gold Star'; with *Selaginella apoda* beneath.

7 This goldfish bowl has been planted with
Ficus pumila.

8 (below) An aquarium offers plenty of scope
for 'landscaping'. This one makes use of rocks
and water as a setting for the plants.

9 An open aquarium gives the chance to see
the plants more clearly, and provides an
opportunity to use a wide range of plants. This
collection includes succulents, bromeliads,
and even a leaf cactus and a hardy rock plant.

10 (far left) This attractive terrarium has been planted with 'air plant' tillandsias, and will require very little attention.

11 (left) The flowers of *Rosa chinensis* give a welcome touch of colour to a terrarium, but of course as with most flowering plants the display is relatively short-lived.

12 (opposite below) Some plants suitable for a bottle garden. Top row, l. to r.: *Codiaeum* 'Gold Star', *Helxine soleirolii, Cryptanthus acaulis, Sansevieria trifasciata* 'Hahnii Variegata', *Cryptanthus acaulis, Chamaedorea elegans.* Middle row (l. to r.): *Fittonia verschaffeltii* 'Argyroneura', *Peperomia caperata, P. clusiifolia* 'Jeli', and *Fittonia verschaffeltii.* Bottom row (l. to r.): *Pilea involucrata, P. spruceana, Fittonia verschaffeltii* 'Argyroneura Nana', *Pilea cadierei,* pilea hybrid.

13 (above right) Some ferns suitable for bottle gardens. Top row (l. to r.): *Pteris cretica* 'Albolineata', adiantum sp., adiantum sp. Middle row (l. to r.): *Nephrolepis exaltata, Pellea rotundifolia, Asplenium nidus.* Bottom row (l. to r.): *Cyrtomium falcatum,* didymochlaena sp., *Pteris cretica.*

14 (centre right) Selaginellas and small-leaved ivies grow well in bottle gardens.

15 (below right) A pleasant selection of plants for, say, a carboy. Back row (l. to r.): *Pteris cretica* 'Cristata', *Euonymus japonicus,* adiantum sp., didymochlaena sp. Middle row: small-leaved ivies and *Nephrolepis exaltata.* Front row (l. to r.): *Selaginella apoda, S. krausiana* 'Aurea' (rear), *Cryptanthus acaulis* (fore), *S. martensii.*

16 (opposite above) The gold and silver forms of *Helxine soleirolii,* hedera, *Codiaeum* 'Gold Star', euonymus, and *Peperomia clusiifolia* 'Jeli'.

17 (opposite below) Some flowering plants that can be used in a suitable open container – kalanchoe, saintpaulia, and nertera (bead plant).

18 (above right) *Chamaedorea elegans, Blechnum gibbum,* and *Cordyline terminalis* 'Red Edge'.

19 (centre right) *Peperomia caperata, Cryptantbus acaulis, Ficus pumila,* and vriesia.

20 (below right) *Dracaena marginata* 'Tricolor'.

21 (top left) Fittonias are useful bottle plants. The red-veined plant is *F. verschaffeltii*, the white-veined one *F. v.* 'Argyroneura', with the smaller *F. v.* 'Argyroneura Nana' in front.

22 (below left) Hypocyrta – a rather straggly plant, but useful if you want a flowering plant in a suitable open container.

23 (top right) Pileas are only suitable for open bottles. These are (clockwise from the back) *P. cadierei, P. spruceana*, and *P. involucrata*.

24 (below right) Three useful selaginellas for bottles (left to right from the back): *S. martensii, S. krausiana* 'Aurea', and *S. apoda*.

5. PLANTING

Your bottles are likely to be much more successful if you plant with care and have everything ready before you start, including all the plants. However good a plan seems on paper, you will not know whether it will work until you have the plants together. In Chapter 7 there are some planting suggestions, but if your maidenhair fern is 30cm (1ft) across when you buy it the chances are you will have to change your plan. Always be prepared to modify your ideas when you have the actual plants in front of you; only then can you judge how they will balance with each other and within the container.

Suitable plants are described in Chapter 6, but as well as plants you need the right tools (which you can make) and the right compost.

COMPOST

Peat-based composts are clean to handle, do not make a planted bottle too heavy, and are generally free from weed seeds and diseases (important at any time, but more so in a sealed bottle). They have many advantages over a loam-based compost, and in a closed container the fact that they are more difficult than a loam-based compost to water correctly does not matter once the atmosphere has been 'balanced'.

There are two major drawbacks. In a very open container with no drainage you will have to be very careful not to over- or under-water, and a loam-based compost such as a John Innes potting compost (No. 1 should be adequate) will be easier to manage. The other problem is the limited reserve of nutrients in peat-based composts.

You could enrich the compost with slow-release fertilisers. There are various kinds. It is best to choose one that you can mix in with the compost; granules that you sprinkle on the surface can look unsightly. You could use pellets that you push into the compost beside the plants.

You will not be able to use regular liquid feeding in a sealed bottle garden, as the compost would soon become waterlogged.

The low long-term nutrient levels of peat-based composts are not such a serious drawback as you would think. You do *not* want your bottle garden plants to grow too vigorously. The more they are fed, the sooner you are likely to have to prune or replant. Be prepared to feed if the plants are looking sickly (though remember this could just be poor light), but do not overfeed.

Commercially prepared bottle gardens are likely to contain a seed compost, or other low-nutrient compost, to keep the plants small for as long as possible (incidentally, dwarfing chemicals are being developed for commercial growers to spray over their bottle garden plants to further stunt their growth, at least in the short term).

For containers with a wide neck, such as a goldfish bowl, a loam-based compost may be easier to manage. You could use a mixture of John Innes potting compost No. 1 and a peat-based potting compost. Be guided, too, by the plants that you will be growing. Succulents such as *Sansevieria trifasciata* 'Hahnii' and bromeliads such as cryptanthus are likely to do better in a loam-based compost or a mixture. The more open, and probably drier, compost around the neck of the plant will reduce the chances of rotting. If you want to grow ferns, however, a peat-based compost is likely to be more successful — *provided you do not let it dry out.*

TOOLS AND AIDS

Improvisation is the key to grappling with the intricacies of planting and maintaining a bottle garden. You can buy indoor tools such as miniature forks and trowels, but they are unlikely to have handles that are long enough, and if they do the chances are you could make something more efficient yourself at a less cost.

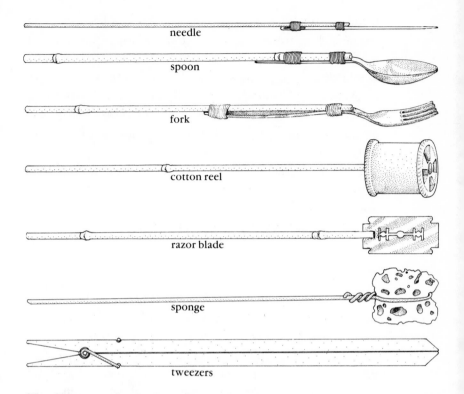

The different tools which may be required for planting and aftercare.

If you are using wide-necked bottles there is an amazing amount that you can do with your hands and fingers, more quickly and more efficiently than messing about with tools for the sake of 'doing it properly'. Do not be afraid to use your hands whenever possible; if you can get your fist in you will be able to scoop a hole, then position and firm in a plant with one hand quite easily and much more quickly than using tools. If it is a dead or diseased leaf that has to be removed, it is much better to pinch it off between your fingers than fiddle about with razor blades on canes (you then have to remove the bit that you have cut off).

Some of the planting illustrations in this book show tools being used even though in some cases it would be possible to insert a small hand, in order to demonstrate the principles whatever the type of bottle you want to plant.

Sometimes, if the container has a narrow neck, you will have no choice but to improvise some tools; and even then you will be taxed on occasion to get what seems an unreasonably large root or amount of foliage through what seems an incredibly small hole.

The tools are not difficult to make, and will cost very little financially or in time. You should be able to find most of the materials lying around the house and garden.

The tools that you will need are listed below.

Firmer

This is an important tool. It is useful for firming the compost before and after planting, but is particularly useful for ensuring that the plants are securely planted, and it is handy for pushing the plant off the scoop or fork and into the hole. If you use a fork to do this there is the frustrating likelihood of impaling the plant and then having to extricate it from the fork with another tool (made difficult in a confined space by the curvature of the fork!).

Make it by pushing an empty cotton bobbin onto the end of a thin garden cane. The only difficulty is finding a cane of the right thickness to fit into the hole and hold the bobbin firmly. You may need to pare the end of a cane slightly to ensure a snug fit.

Fork

This is useful for all kinds of jobs, not only acting as one half of a 'claw' for holding plants. You can use it as a 'spear' to hold a plant while you insert it. You can use it for spiking things to lift out if they are out of reach (dead leaves for instance). You can use it for loosening the surface of the compost during maintenance.

Make it by lashing on an old kitchen fork to a thin garden cane (see p. 35). Try to avoid one with a pronounced curve at the 'blunt' end; it will hold the stem away from the cane and make the lashing more difficult to secure properly.

Scoop

A spoon will double as a trowel or scoop. A desert spoon is a practical size, but for a very narrow-necked container you may need to resort to a teaspoon. It will be perfectly satisfactory, just a little more fiddly.

Make it by lashing to a thin garden cane, as with the fork. Again, try to avoid one with a curved lip to the end of the handle, otherwise it will be difficult to secure firmly against the cane.

Tweezers

These can be used for picking out dead leaves or even improvised tools that have disintegrated in use! They are far from essential, however, and the problems of manipulating them to the place you want, in a narrow-necked bottle, is not easy.

Make them by taking two thin strips of wood about 25cm (10in) long (make them long enough to reach comfortably to the compost but not needlessly long), and use the spring from a spring-loaded peg to provide the pincer action.

Plane or file the ends of the pieces of wood to approximately the same angle as the V-shaped ends of the peg. Remove the spring from the peg (hold one half of the peg firmly and twist the other half — the spring should come out easily). Make notches in your new wood to match *those used for the spring* in the peg. You can use saw cuts or round wood files. Insert the peg spring in one piece, place the second one on top, pulling one end of the spring to one side, and let it click into place.

There are other ways of making long tweezers, including elastic bands for springs, and you may find these easier; this is one of the tools where individual skills dictate which is the easiest to make and the most convenient to use. If the whole thing sounds too much trouble, you could also try using two pieces of wood like chopsticks to remove the offending item!

Sponge

This is really useful for cleaning the glass. Bits of compost often cling to the glass no matter how careful you are when planting, and most of these can be removed with a sponge. Syringeing the glass clean or trickling water down it is effective, but there is a limit to how much water you can use without waterlogging the compost. Using a sponge on a wire you should be able to reach any part of the container.

To make it tie a piece of sponge (plastic 'foam' will do if you do not have a piece of real sponge to spare) to a piece of stiff wire; try to twist the wire around the sponge for extra security. The wire should be flexible enough to bend under pressure but stiff enough to stay in the position set.

Spike

This is useful for spearing loose leaves or adjusting the way stems or leaves are lying within the container (be careful not to spear them).

The most convenient and effective method of making it is to use a mounted needle that you can tie to a cane. Failing that you could insert a darning needle into the end of a thin cane (you may have to saw the cane across at a node (joint) to ensure that there is enough solid tissue to hold the needle.

A word of warning. Do make sure that all your home-made tools are firmly secured to the canes. Do not assume they cannot fall off in use — they can. Having a bobbin, a razor blade, or anything else, to fish out if you have nearly completed your garden is frustrating and taxing to say the least.

Scalpel

If you plant your garden carefully, drastic surgery should not be necessary, but most of us tend to use some plants that are a little too vigorous (we want to see something substantial growing quickly), and even the best-kept bottles need attention at some time. Using a sharp blade will enable you to cut leaves and stems off cleanly, which will reduce the chance of diseases taking hold.

To make it you could strap a proper scalpel to a cane, but you are more likely to have a razor blade about the house. Make a thin slit in the bottom of a cane and slot the blade into this. It is important that the blade is a tight fit (careful of fingers when pushing it in), otherwise pressure in use may dislodge the blade. There will be less chance of this happening if you use a sawing motion with little pressure, rather than cutting through a stem with a thrusting action.

HOW TO PLANT

Whether you make a clear glass terrarium with no access problems, or a garden in a carboy or bottle with a narrow neck, the principles are the same; only the method of planting varies. You will need the following items.

1) Pea gravel. Coarse grit will do if gravel is not available.
2) Horticultural charcoal. You should be able to buy this from a garden centre; alternatively you should be able to obtain suitable charcoal from an aquarium shop — it is used in filters.
3) Compost. See p. 33.
4) Stiff paper or card to make a funnel.
5) A piece of paper cut to the size of the container (if a tapering bottle, the size of the widest part that the plants will occupy),
6) A collection of suitable plants. See Chapter 6.
7) Suitable tools. A comprehensive list was given on pp. 36-9, but you can manage with just an improvised fork, scoop and tamper. If you can get your hands into the container easily you will not even need these.

Planting a carboy or bottle

1) Using a funnel to keep the sides of the container clean, spread

a 2.5-5cm (1-2in) layer of gravel over the bottom. Add a thin layer of charcoal.

2) Still using the funnel, add about 5cm (2in) of compost, and use the tamper to ensure that it is spread evenly and firmed gently. If you are to look at the bottle mainly from one angle, there is no harm in banking the compost up at one side if you want a more 'landscaped' effect.

3) Select the plants that you think will look right, and arrange them on the paper or card that you have cut out to the diameter of the bottle or container. None of the plants should overlap the edge — any that do will touch the glass, something to avoid as the leaves may rot and it means that the plants will have little scope for extra growth.

4) The plants should be in small pots, no larger than 7.5cm (3in), ideally only 6cm (2½in). If you can insert the root-ball through the hole without removing the compost from the roots, *do so*. It is sometimes recommended that the roots are washed free of the old compost, but it is an unnecessary check to the plant if you do not need to do it. It may be necessary to reduce the depth of the root-ball because of the shallow layer of compost. Simply untease the roots at the bottom and knock away some of the compost, keeping the top intact.

Preparing to plant: step 3.

Steps 1–3

Step 4

Step 5

Step 6

41

Planting a wide-necked bottle: step 5.

5) Start planting at the outside and work towards the centre. Scoop out a hole in the compost, matching the position on the layout, and lower the plant into place. If the neck of the container is not too narrow you can do this by hand. If there is not enough room, lower it in between scoop (spoon) and fork. You may even be able to push the prongs of the fork into the root-ball and lower it in this way (if you do not manage to shake it free when it is in position, push it off the fork with the tamper).

If the neck is very narrow, or the plant larger than usual, you may have no option but to wash the roots free of compost. Even then you will have to be very careful how you push the roots through the narrow neck; avoid squeezing them. Once the roots are through, ease the leaves through as gently as possible, then firm into place carefully. It may help to roll the leaves in a small square of polythene so that you can feed them through the neck as a 'tube'. Keep hold of the top of the polythene. The leaves should spring back into place once the polythene is pulled free. If there is a lot of foliage that makes firming in difficult in the restricted area, you should be able to shake the compost into place over most of the roots provided you made a suitable depression to start with and the compost is banked around the sides. You may not be able to cover all the roots, but in the closed environment of a bottle garden new roots soon form and many plants recover quite easily from treatment that might normally have killed them.

Planting a narrow-necked bottle: step 5.

6) Once the bottle has been planted, either trickle water down the inside of the glass (to clean the glass while watering), or mist with a compression sprayer, again directing the spray to clean the glass. *Do not overwater.* This is the most critical stage of making your bottle garden or terrarium — do not underestimate its importance. Even if you are not planting a sealed bottle, moisture will take much longer to evaporate than it would from pots in an unprotected atmosphere. If you overwater now, the plants could be killed. At best you are

likely to lose plants from diseases and rots. Add very little water initially; you can add more later if necessary.

7) If the glass still needs cleaning (bits of compost have a knack of sticking to moist glass), wipe it with the sponge on a wire.

GETTING IT BALANCED

A sealed bottle will have to be 'balanced'. Too little water and the plants will suffer; too much and even before the plants succumb you will lose the benefit of your bottle because of the constant condensation.

There is no short-cut or substitute for a little trial and error. If the compost looks too wet, do not insert the stopper; wait until the compost looks just moist then insert the stopper.

It is normal for the bottle to mist up inside when the outside temperature drops and the moisture in the atmosphere within the bottle condenses on the cold glass. It is likely to be a problem in the mornings, but should soon clear as the day progresses if you have used a glass container (it tends to cling to plastic rather than running down it).

If there is *no* condensation, the compost is probably too dry and may need a *little* more water. If the condensation does not clear, or if it is particularly heavy, the compost is almost certainly too wet. Remove the stopper for a few days, then try again.

If the condensation seems particularly heavy, try absorbing some of it with a sponge fixed to a wire (see p. 35). This will speed up the process of losing excess water; even if the top of a bottle is left open condensation will still form and a significant proportion of the moisture will be returned to the compost. The sooner excess moisture is lost, the better.

Be prepared to make these minor adjustments until the bottle is balanced: compost just moist, but not wet; some condensation forming on most days, but clearing.

6. THE PLANTS

No list of plants can really be complete. There are always more possibilities than it is possible to include, and you will inevitably come across the odd unusual species that would be suitable but is too uncommon to merit inclusion in a general list.

Almost all the plants mentioned in this book are available from good garden centres with a strong pot-plant collection. Many pot plants are imported, and supply may be spasmodic; you are unlikely to be able to buy all the plants mentioned at any one time, but if you are near some good garden centres you should be able to obtain them during the course of say a year. Sadly, they may not all be labelled (or at least not with the species or varieties), so it can be difficult if you do not know what the plants look like.

Generally, wild plants have been avoided, because it is not a good idea to go out collecting unless you really know your plants, and because it is frustrating to be told of some super native fern if you live in a city and have little chance of finding it. Common mosses are the exception — you can find them in most places, and you are unlikely to do much harm by collecting them.

The plants mentioned have the merit of being reasonably easy to buy if you shop around, and dependable enough in a bottle garden to give you a good chance of success (though some will still need care to keep them compact and in good health over a long period). If you see some other plant that looks equally promising, do not be afraid to experiment; especially if you have gained a little experience with known bottle garden plants. But be prepared for disappointments. There are a few plants regularly sold for bottle gardens (and even in planted bottles) that are far from ideal. Some of these have been included under 'Plants to Avoid' on page 62.

WHAT TO LOOK FOR WHEN YOU BUY

Always buy small plants: they will give you more months of pleasure before they become too large, and will be easier to manipulate and plant. A plant in a 10cm (4in) pot is likely to have a root-ball about 7cm (3in) deep — far too large to plant without removing most of the compost. A small plant will transplant more easily, and in many containers you will probably be able to keep most of the root-ball intact.

'Tots' in about 5-6cm (2-2½in) pots are admirably suited. They are little more than rooted cuttings or young plants grown from seed, but cheap and perfectly adequate for a bottle garden. They are often displayed for sale in mixed trays, and may be labelled as 'suitable for bottle gardens'; many are, but be cautious as some are likely to be unsuitable.

Unfortunately, 'tots' do not normally have labels if they are sold in mixed trays. Unless you know a particular plant, it may be best to give it a miss.

Plants a little larger, in 7.5cm (3in) pots, are likely to be labelled in a good garden centre or shop, and you will probably have a wider choice of species. These are fine for bottle gardens, although you may have to remove some of the compost from the root-ball. Some, such as selaginellas, can often be divided into several smaller pieces.

Larger plants, in say 10cm (4in) pots, can be used in large containers, or where you want instant impact and are prepared for the much more fiddly job of getting them into a container with a narrow neck. In an aquarium, however, a larger specimen will be relatively easy to plant.

If you want a flowering plant, you may have to accept a fairly large specimen. As you will probably be looking on these as a short-term decoration anyway, simply be guided by the size of your container.

Whatever the size, be pernickety about the *quality* of the plant. Pests are a nuisance at any time, but are more difficult to deal with in a bottle garden, and a crushed, damaged, or yellowing leaf that would normally have little effect on the rest of the plant can be disastrous if it starts rotting in an enclosed container. The plants must also be compact and bushy, because if they are leggy beforehand they will never make a good plant in a bottle.

If you are buying in winter, always keep the plant well wrapped on the way home ... and do not buy plants that have been standing outside the shop in the cold. A cold shock may not have an immediately obvious effect, but you could find that the leaves start to drop several days later, especially with sensitive plants such as crotons.

PLANTS FOR A STOPPERED BOTTLE

All these can also be used in an unsealed bottle, but those with an asterisk are likely to do better in the closer, more humid atmosphere of a sealed bottle.

Adiantum spp.* (Plate 13)

MAIDENHAIR FERN   Maidenhair ferns are widely available and do well in a large bottle garden. They make fairly large and bushy plants, however, and are often most effective by themselves. Given space to arch out in graceful sprays, they are extremely graceful. Several forms are likely to be found in shops, some very similiar and others distinctive but probably simply labelled 'Adiantum'.

All of them have sprays of dainty pale green fan-shaped leaflets on wiry-looking stems. Most will grow to about 20-30cm (8-12in).

Adiantum raddianum (syn. *A. cuneatum*) and *A. capillus-veneris* are very similar. There are various varieties, unlikely to be named on the label. It is worth looking out for *A. c-v.* 'Imbricatum', which has overlapping, frilly-looking leaves that are particularly attractive and more showy; there is also a variety with very small, frail, extremely delicate leaves that really needs the benefit of a sealed atmosphere. *A. r.* 'Fragrantissimum' (you may find it labelled as *A. fragrans*) has sweet-smelling fronds; but

47

this is hardly a plus point if the plant is in a bottle.

If all the names seem confusing, do not worry. Any of the adiantums that you find on sale in shops are likely to make good bottle garden plants, provided that you allow space for the arching stems.

Propagation   Best to buy plants, although it is worth trying to divide an old plant if you are replanting a bottle.

Asplenium nidus

BIRD'S NEST FERN   A distinctive if untypical fern, forming a rosette of entire (undivided), sword-like leaves. These glossy, light green leaves are arranged vase-like, unfurling from the centre of the rosette. Useful because its upright habit and shape add interest, but it will outgrow most bottles in about a year (a good specimen can have leaves 1m (3ft) long, though only after time and in suitable conditions). Useful for very large bottles or as a short-term plant in a smaller one. Choose a *small* plant.

Propagation   Best to buy a plant; small ones are not expensive.

Asplenium tricomanes

MAIDENHAIR SPLEENWORT   This native British fern is common in rock and masonry crevices. It is included despite the general policy of not including wild plants because it is an abundant fern in Britain and many other countries, and is also available from fern specialists if you do not want to rape the country-side. It grows 5-15cm (2-6in) high, which makes it an ideal bottle garden plant.

Propagation   Best to buy a plant, or you may even have one growing in your garden.

Blechnum (Plate 18)

Blechnum penna-marina is a very desirable bottle garden fern, but you may have to go to a fern specialist to buy it. It grows to about 5-10cm (2-4in) high, unlike some other species that are far too large to consider. You might find *B. gibbum* in shops and garden centres, which could be used in a reasonably large container. The deeply cut fronds form a closely-knit spiral on top of an erect stem, giving it a somewhat palm-like shape.

Propagation For *B. gibbum* it is best to buy a new plant produced commercially. You should be able to divide *B. penna-marina* satisfactorily.

Chamaedorea elegans (Plate 18)

PARLOUR PALM   The concept of a palm in a bottle may seem incongruous. Yet because the parlour palm is compact and slow-growing it can make an interesting bottle garden feature for several years. It is, of course, best in a container with generous height. The light, feathery foliage is held on slightly arching upright stems — a miniature palm in every way. Even quite young plants flower; yellow, mimosa-like flowers can appear on plants only 45cm (18in) high. These may be followed by pea-like berries. Although many palms are expensive, young plants of this easy-to-grow species are unlikely to cost you any more than most other plants in this list. You may find this palm sold under the name *Neanthe bella*.

Propagation   Best to buy plants. Can be raised from seed, but it is much quicker and easier to buy a plant.

Cocos weddeliana

DWARF COCONUT PALM   Another palm that can make a surprisingly good bottle garden plant. It is a slow-growing plant, and if you select a small one it will be relatively inexpensive and also give you a year or two of use in the bottle. Even though it is slow-growing, you should use a container that is large enough to allow its fronds to arch gracefully without being cramped. Sometimes this cocos is sold with several to a pot (to make a better initial display). As root disturbance is resented, plant the group without disturbance if the container is large enough.

Propagation   Best left to the professionals with suitable facilities.

Codiaeum 'Gold Star' (Plate 16)

CROTON   Most codiaeums are unsuitable for container gardens.

They are generally large-leaved plants that are far too large. The variety 'Gold Star' is smaller and more compact, with small, narrow, strap-like yellow and green leaves much more suitable for a container. All crotons can be difficult to grow, and it is best to get the plant established in the summer rather than buy one during the cold and dull winter months.

Propagation You can take cuttings, but it is unlikely that a plant in a bottle garden would be large enough for this, and they are not easy to root in the home. Best to buy plants.

Cryptanthus (Plate 19)

EARTH STAR   In many ways ideal plants for bottle gardens and terrariums: low-growing, interesting shape, leaves with useful colour and variegation, and slow-growing. There are many species and varieties, varying in size and colouring. Avoid the larger species and hybrids unless the container is large, and choose the small *C. acaulis*. Do not be too influenced by colour — it may change! In good light the colouring usually contains warm pinks and reds, yet the same plant will become more cream and green after it has been in poor light. Some species and hybrids are more colourful in any light.

Propagation Best to buy plants.

Ficus pumila (Plate 19)

CREEPING FIG   Not everyone's idea of an attractive plant — its small, oval, plain green leaves are unspectacular. Its attraction lies in the creeping habit; in a hanging container it will trail, in a bottle garden or terrarium it will creep. Useful for a 'ground cover' as a foil for more upright plants, but it can be rather vigorous. Its small size and tolerance of poor light make it suitable for growing in quite difficult places, such as a wine bottle. There is a variegated form; this can be more demanding in the home, but it should succeed in a bottle garden. It is easy to confuse *F. pumila* (Plate 7) with *F. radicans*, though this plant has slightly larger and more oval leaves. You could use this instead. There is also a variegated form of this species.

Propagation   Easy to raise from cuttings rooted in summer.

Fittonia verschaffeltii 'Argyroneura Nana'*
(Plates 12 and 21)

SNAKESKIN PLANT   Three fittonias are likely to be found in shops and garden centres: the red-veined *F. verschaffeltii*, silver-veined *F. v.* 'Argyroneura', and the similar but much smaller *F. v.*. 'Argyroneura Nana'. Out of this cacophony of tongue-twisting names, 'Nana' is the key word meaning 'dwarf'. The leaves on this plant are only about 2cm long, whereas the larger kinds have leaves about 8cm long. Unless the bottle is large, choose the small, more compact 'Nana'. It is a charming plant. You may find 'Argyroneura' and 'Argyroneura Nana' labelled as *F. argyroneura* and *F. a.* 'Nana' respectively.
Propagation   The creeping stems will probably have rooted on their own; you should be able to divide the plant when you replant the bottle.

Hedera helix (Plates 14 and 16)

IVY   Ivies need no introduction — they are versatile plants with varieties suitable for covering a wall outdoors and for providing ground cover in a bottle garden. There is plenty of variation in both leaf shape and colour, so it should not be difficult to find one that suits. Most of the *small-leaved* varieties of *Hedera helix* can be used, but avoid large-leaved ivies, especially *H. canariensis* 'Gloire de Marengo', which is a popular pot plant.

The chances are the varieties will not be named when you buy your ivies, but if they are, some good names to look out for are 'Glacier', 'Gold Child', 'Little Eva', and 'Lutzii'. You should be able to buy several with yellow or white variegation, but do not overlook leaf *shape*. Leaf shape and growth habit can add as much to your arrangement as colour.

Helxine soleirolii (Plate 16)

MIND YOUR OWN BUSINESS, BABY'S TEARS   You may also find this plant under its more recent name of *Soleirolia soleirolii*. It

51

has what appear to be all the qualities of a good bottle garden plant. It has low, compact growth, fresh appearance, colour variations (there are golden and silver forms), and a delicate charm on a par with many of the selaginellas.

Unfortunately it has drawbacks as a bottle plant: it can be a rampant grower and may smother some of the more delicate plants. It also has a habit of dying off in a sealed bottle garden. Once a soft, fleshy plant like this starts to rot it can be a disaster in a closed environment. Nevertheless well worth growing, especially in an open container.

The small, rounded leaves are carried on thin fragile-looking stems. Growth is perky and upright if growing healthily and undisturbed, but easily damaged by prodding and crushing. The gold and silver forms are much more attractive than the green form for clear glass, but the green one is just as good for a green glass container and may do better in the poor light.

Propagation Clumps root as they spread; simply divide into smaller pieces when you replant.

Maranta

PRAYER PLANT, HERRINGBONE PLANT, PEACOCK PLANT (DEPENDING ON SPECIES) The four marantas that you are likely to find in shops are all useful bottle garden plants: *M. leuconeura* 'Kerchoveana' (the prayer plant) has dark brown-black blotches on the leaves; *M. l.* 'Erythrophylla' (the herringbone plant, known also as *M. tricolor*) has attractive pinkish-red veins; *M. l.* 'Massageana' is similar but with silvery white veins; *M. makoyana* (more correctly *Calathea makoyana*) is a larger plant with white and green leaves, suitable for a large bottle (the other species mentioned do not normally grow larger than 20-25cm/8-10in). The leaves tend to fold up at night, and this is particularly striking with *M. leuconeura* 'Kerchoveana'; the leaves stand upright and folded in darkness, which gives rise to the common name of prayer plant.

Propagation An established plant can be divided when replanting the bottle.

Nephrolepis exaltata (Plates 13 and 15)

LADDER FERN, SWORD FERN Can make a large, magnificent specimen far too large for a bottle, but so attractive that it is worth including a small plant even if you have to replace it at the end of the year (promote the old one to a pot and you will have a handsome pot plant). The arching, pale green fronds have the leaflets arranged ladder-like; with some varieties the fronds are more divided and ruffled. If you are fortunate you may be able to obtain a dwarf variety such as 'Childsii', though probably only from a specialist.

Propagation In spring new plantlets may be produced on runners. These can be separated to produce new plants.

Pellaea rotundifolia (Plate 13)

BUTTON FERN Not particularly fern-like in appearance, and lacking the gracefulness of most ferns, but nevertheless a useful plant. Its low habit means that it is useful as a 'ground cover' in most containers; but bear in mind that its spreading, rather floppy habit can give even a young plant a spread of 15cm (6in). As the common name of button fern implies, the leaflets are round and button-shaped. The colour is a rather dark green, but the plant provides an interesting variation in shape and appearance among the ferns.

Propagation Best to buy plants.

Peperomia spp. (Plate 16)

You will find a wide range of peperomias in shops and garden centres, but few of them are suitable for an enclosed bottle garden. As a general rule, those with crinkly leaves and freely-produced (albeit insignificant) flower spikes are best in an unstoppered bottle; for a sealed container choose those with glossy, smooth leaves. *P. magnoliifolia* 'Variegata', the desert privet, with its boldly variegated green and cream leaves is a popular choice and easy to find. *P. m.* 'USA' is similar. The leaves are fleshy, rounded in outline. *P. clusiifolia jeli*, with its larger more oval and richly-coloured leaves suffused purple-pink is not so common but is worth considering for a large container if you find it.

Propagation Cuttings rooted in summer.

Pteris spp. (Plates 13 and 15)

Some of the most popular indoor ferns. Most of them are suitable if the container is large enough, but for small bottles it is best to keep to some of the more compact variegated varieties.

Pteris cretica, the ribbon fern, which has deeply branched and divided fronds, is usually represented by one of the varieties with more heavily crested tips to the leaflets. 'Cristata' is one of these.

P. c. 'Albolineata', has a white central line running down each pinnae (section of the leaf).

P. ensiformis 'Victoriae', has heavily silvered leaves, is a rather more graceful fern, and perhaps more suitable for a bottle garden or fern case. If you see one labelled *P. e.* 'Evergemiensis', this is an even more desirable form with better variegation.

Propagation Best raised from cuttings, though you might be able to divide an old plant when replanting a bottle.

Syngonium 'White Butterfly'

GOOSEFOOT PLANT Only suitable for a large container, the arrowhead leaves of this normally climbing or trailing plant are variegated cream and green. Actually leaf shape can change as the plant matures. For a large bottle, however, the striking leaves and spreading habit can make a strong impact even when newly planted.

Propagation Cuttings can usually be rooted in summer.

Selaginella spp.* (Plates 14 and 24)

CREEPING MOSS Selaginellas are among the best sealed bottle garden plants. They thrive in the enclosed atmosphere, and their generally compact habit also makes them ideal.

There are several species that you might find at garden centres, all of them resembling large mosses. They are usually unlabelled, or simply identified as 'selaginella' with no species given. It does not matter — they are all suitable, and have a place in the bottle garden, though some need a larger container than others. *Selaginella apoda* forms small green hummocks a few centimetres (inches) high; it is a feathery, moss-like plant, but in the author's experience more difficult to grow than the other species mentioned. Much coarser in growth and more upright is *S. martensii*; both this and the white-splashed *S. m.* 'Watsoniana' will reach 25cm (10in) and need a large bottle or a container with adequate height. *S. krausiana* 'Aurea' is a real charmer. It forms a loose golden mound. Delicate and cheerful.

Propagation Cuttings root easily in summer. In a humid atmosphere roots hang down from the stems anyway and it is easy to break into rooted pieces.

Vriesea splendens (Plate 19)

FLAMING SWORD   If you have ever seen one of these in flower, with its long, orange-red flowering spike (the actual flowers are small and fairly insignificant, it is the bracts that are vividly coloured), you will wonder how this plant could possibly be suggested for a bottle garden. The plants usually sold as 'bottle garden tots' are in fact seedlings that will take years (as well as skill and the right conditions) to grow to flowering size.

In the meantime, their distinctive vase shape and dark-banded leaves can provide a useful contrast of shape and texture. They are not a long-term bottle plant; a couple of years may be all you will get out of one, but that is as long as many others will last without pruning or replanting. Worth considering provided you do not expect the striking blooms that you see on mature plants.

SOME PLANTS FOR OPEN BOTTLES

Acorus gramineus 'Variegatus'

SWEET FLAG   This grass-like plant is sometimes used in bottles, and it adds another variation of shape and habit. The narrow leaves have off-white stripes. Particularly useful to plant at the edge of a miniature pool in say a converted aquarium, or where you need a plant with an upright, tufty habit.

Propagation   Divide the plants at any time of year.

Aglaeonema

Included with reservations. Can be impressive as a centrepiece for a *large* bottle, but generally likely to be out of proportion. There are many species and varieties that you might encounter; most of them can be used provided you are willing to move them on once they become too large for the container. Most of them have attractively marked foliage, usually splashed with silver or yellow, and a 'tufty' habit of growth.

Propagation   Remove suckers or rooted basal shoots in early summer.

Cordyline

Most cordylines are too large for a bottle garden, but *C. terminalis* 'Red Edge' makes a striking centrepiece for a large bottle and should provide many months of pleasure before it outgrows its welcome. The richly coloured red-edged, purple-green leaves are smaller than the ordinary species and most other varieties, so try to make sure that you buy this variety.

Propagation   Not easy. Probably best to remove the plant and put it into a pot, then air layer to start off again with a more compact plant.

Cyrtomium falcatum (Plate 13)

HOLLY FERN   The common name aptly describes the shape of the dark, glossy green leaves. This tough fern will do well in the home even outside the protection of a bottle. Once it is growing well it can make quite coarse, spreading growth, so you may need to trim to shape if necessary.

Propagation   Divide an established plant when replanting.

Dieffenbachia 'Compacta'

DUMB CANE, LEOPARD LILY   Another plant that will eventually make a large specimen, but worth considering for a large bottle because of its striking cream and green foliage. There are other varieties, including a particularly bright one with mainly cream leaves called 'Camilla', but you will need to choose a small plant. Be cautious with the sap: do not get it into your mouth as it can cause serious irritation.

Propagation A section of stem can be cut up into pieces about 5-7.5cm (2-3in) long, and just covered with compost. You will need to do this in summer unless you have a heated propagator. If the plant is large you may be able to remove a small offset from the base, but a bottle garden plant is not likely to be big enough for this.

Dracaena (Plate 20)

Two dracaenas have to be mentioned, *D. marginata* and *D. sanderiana*. *Dracaena marginata* 'Tricolor' will grow as a head on a tall stem, but young plants make such a striking centrepiece that it is hard to resist including it for a clear bottle where you can appreciate the narrow green, cream and red leaves. The small low-growing head that you will need to use may be described as a 'tip', to distinguish it from those grown on a leg (but remember that your tip will eventually grow tall too).

In good conditions in the home, *D. sanderiana* will reach 1m (3ft) and can be quite bushy. It is much smaller if the roots are contained, but still only a plant to use for a limited period. Useful as a centrepiece in a large bottle. The broad, strap-shaped leaves are edged with a broad white band.

Propagation Not easy. You may be able to air layer a leggy plant (take it out of the bottle first), or use pieces of stem as cane cuttings.

Euonymus japonicus (Plate 16)

If you know this plant as a large hardy shrub in the garden, it may seem an unlikely candidate for a bottle garden. The two varieties usually grown as indoor pot plants are *E. j.* 'Ovatus Aureus' (gold and green leaves) and *E. j.* 'Microphyllus' (smaller, green and white leaves). Although these are naturally compact varieties, they will still grow rapidly. Pinch out the growing tip if the plant is not naturally bushy, and be prepared to replace the plant after perhaps a year.

Useful because of their upright habit, but neither plant looks as good in a coloured bottle as it does out. The bold variegation, especially on 'Ovatus Aureus', soon pales in the poor light, and much of the impact is lost. You will also be able to appreciate the variegation better through an open-topped bottle, or a sealed bottle made from clear glass. Do not be deterred from trying this plant because it will outgrow the container; you can plant it in the garden afterwards, and you will have bought a nice garden shrub for the price of a 'tot'.

Propagation Stem cuttings can be rooted in summer. Once rooted, grow the plants on in good light for a few months before using in the bottle garden again.

Fittonia (Plates 12 and 21)

SILVER NET LEAF, PAINTED NET LEAF   The small-leaved kind has already been described for sealed bottles. There are two other fittonias that you could use: *F. verschaffeltii* 'Argyroneura' and *F. verschaffeltii* itself. Do not let the names put you off buying them. Neither are easy as ordinary house plants, but will grow well in a protected, humid environment. The reason for not including these in the sealed bottle list is because their large leaves and somewhat ungainly sprawling habit usually calls for some judicious 'pruning' from time to time. *F. verschaffeltii* 'Argyroneura' (silver net leaf) has green leaves with striking silvery-white veins. *F. verschaffeltii* (painted net leaf) has pinkish-red veins.

Propagation   The creeping stems will probably root themselves. Pot them up as cuttings.

Peperomia (Plate 12)

Some suitable peperomias have already been mentioned for sealed gardens. There are others that are attractive and perfectly

58

suitable for an open bottle; it is simply that they have flower spikes that will eventually need removing, and the old leaves have a habit of dropping and rotting, so you need ready access. Always try to remove the old flower stems as they collapse, and before they have chance to rot. One of the most widely available is *P. caperata*. It has a neat habit, but bear in mind that its flowering spikes (which are creamy, catkin-like pokers) will probably double the height of the plant.

Propagation *P. caperata* can be propagated from individual leaves, inserting the leaf stalk far enough into the compost to keep the leaves erect with the base sitting on the soil.

Pilea (Plate 12 and 23)

ALUMINIUM PLANT, FRIENDSHIP PLANT, MOON VALLEY PLANT (DEPENDING ON SPECIES) The pileas are attractive plants, and they are often included in ready-planted bottle gardens sold in shops and garden centres. The reason is obvious — as young plants grown in good conditions in a nursery, they are neat, compact, and very attractive. Unfortunately they can grow rapidly and all tend to become leggy as well as bigger. Even in good light it is best to keep pinching out the growing tips; in the poorer light of a green bottle in the home it is very difficult to keep them looking good. The answer is to propagate them frequently and replace the plants when they need it. That way you can enjoy them as bottle garden plants, but you need the ready access of an unsealed bottle.

Particularly popular is the aluminium plant, *P. cadierei*, with its silver-splashed leaves, but there are also several other species and their varieties that you may find. *P. involucrata* (friendship plant) has green, crinkly leaves with dark veins and an impressive symmetrical way of growing. *P. mollis* (moon valley plant) is similar, and there are several forms of *P. spruceana*, including 'Norfolk', which has leaves that can be a mixture of purple and silver, though the quality of light makes a significant difference to colouring.

Avoid *P. microphylla* (syn *P. muscosa*) the artillery plant, as this is not really suitable. The others make interesting plants (perhaps as a collection) provided that you realise their limitations and feel that you can cope with the attention that they need. Be prepared for losses during the winter.

Pseuderanthemum atropurpureum

Not a common plant, but worth trying if you find it. The oval leaves are blotched or mottled green, bronze, and pink. The colours are best appreciated in a clear glass container. Good light is in any case important for the plant (though direct sunlight should be avoided). May become 'leggy', so be prepared to replace the plants when necessary.

Propagation You should be able to root cuttings if you have a heated propagator; if you do not have a heated propagator, try rooting them during the summer months, keeping the atmosphere humid.

Sansevieria trifasciata 'Hahnii' (Plate 12)

BIRD'S NEST SANSEVIERIA   The sansevieria that most of us think of when the name is mentioned is mother-in-law's tongue, the ordinary *S. trifasciata*. The bird's nest sansevieria (sometimes sold as *S. hahnii*) is much more compact, growing as a small rosette. The normal plant has green leaves mottled silvery-grey, but there is a particularly attractive variety with gold and green leaves, *S. t.* 'Hahnii Variegata'.

Propagation Remove offsets from established plants.

Tillandsia (Plate 10)

AIR PLANTS   There are two basic types of tillandsia that you should be able to buy: those grown primarily for their flowers, rooted in compost like a conventional plant; and those grown for their interesting shapes and general appearance and which are *not* grown in compost. It is the latter group, popularly known as air plants, that you could use for a terrarium display.

These plants take their moisture from the air, and seem to grow on nothing! They are usually grey in colour, and generally have long narrow leaves that grow as a tuft. Do not mix them with normal bottle-garden plants, as they would almost certainly look incongruous. Because they would look rather ridiculous just lying on the compost, you need to display them artistically, perhaps on twigs and pieces of stone. You can fix them in position with wire or wedge them with pieces of moss, if you are unable to rest the plants in natural crevices.

There are many species, if you want a variety of shapes and forms, but some dependable ones to start with are *T. caput-medusae, T. ionantha. T. i. scaprosa, T. i. longifolia, and T. juncea*. Because they have to take their nutrients from the air, it is best to mist them with water containing a weak liquid fertiliser occasionally during the summer. This is why they have been recommended for this section rather than for a sealed container.

FLOWERING PLANTS

Flowering plants should only be used in containers where it is easy to remove dead flowers. Because flowering plants generally only bloom for a short period it is best to view them as short-term plants. Those that will flower again, such as African violets, are best removed and given more suitable conditions and better light after they have finished blooming; then they are more likely to do well for another year.

Hypocyrta glabra (Plate 22)

CLOG PLANT   A useful plant even when it is not in flower, with glossy, dark green, leaves resembling those of box (*Buxus* spp). It carries its small orange-red flowers over a long period, usually in spring and summer. It often has a lax, almost trailing habit.

Propagation   Divide old plants when replanting, or take stem cuttings after flowering. Pinch out the growing tips of rooted cuttings to encourage a bushy, more compact habit.

Kalanchoe blossfeldiana (Plates 5 and 17)

FLAMING KATY A particularly useful plant because it is available in flower during the winter, and will remain in bloom for many weeks. The habit of modern varieties is also compact and neat. There are red, yellow, and orange shades. If you buy a plant in flower at Christmas and keep it for another year, it will probably flower in spring; commercially they are induced to flower early by altering day length. Old plants tend to become straggly, and it is best to use fresh, compact plants for your display.

Propagation Can be raised from seed, but cuttings are easy to root from late spring to summer.

Saintpaulia (Plate 17)

AFRICAN VIOLET A very popular plant for the home, and effective as a solitary specimen or as a centrepiece in a brandy snifter, or some other decorative container. Best in clear glass so that you can appreciate the flowers. You must be careful to pick off dead flowers regularly and to remove dying or damaged leaves carefully; do not leave stumps that could start to rot.

Propagation Leaf cuttings are easy to root.

Nertera granadensis (Plate 17)

BEAD PLANT The chances are you will find this plant labelled as *N. depressa*; these distinct species are sometimes confused within the trade. A distinctive plant grown for its tightly-packed brilliant orange berries rather than its flowers. It can be kept for another year, if rested in winter and put outdoors for the summer, but is best regarded as an expendable plant for a bottle garden. It is usually available in the autumn, when its berries are at their most attractive.

Propagation Divide plants in spring, but for a bottle garden it is best to buy plants when they are in berry.

PLANTS TO AVOID

Some of the plants already mentioned can be unsuitable if they are too large, but there are two plants that can be particularly deceptive.

The asparagus fern in its various forms — *Asparagus densiflorus* (syn. *A. sprengeri*) and *A. setaceus* (syn. *A. plumosus*) for example — may sound suitable because of the word 'fern' in the common name. In fact they are not ferns, but more importantly they will soon become too large for most containers.

Even more tempting to buy will be the polka dot plant *(Hypoestes sanguinolenta)*. It is widely used in commercially planted bottles, and the plants on sale will look dainty and very compact. They will have been grown in good light, however, and probably have been treated with a dwarfing chemical. This will wear off after a month or so, and in poor light you will soon have a far from attractive plant growing out of the top of the bottle.

7. PLANTING IDEAS

This section of the book is to give you starting points from which to develop your own planting plans. Be careful not to follow any of the plans given here without regard to the size of the container and the size of the plants. Most of the plants given can be bought as small or large specimens, with everything in between; it is possible to buy two specimens of the same plant, say a maidenhair fern, and have one more than four times the size of the other. Be prepared to modify any arrangement to suit the size of the plants that you have available.

It is also unlikely that you will be able to obtain *all* the right plants locally at the same time, and there is no harm in substituting an alternative plant to overcome the problem.

The permutations are almost endless, even with the short list of candidates given in this book. On the one hand this gives you plenty of scope to experiment with different ideas; on the other it can make it difficult to know where to start. It is to give you starting points that the following planting schemes have been included.

Always remember, however, that you should be clear whether you are creating a sealed bottle or terrarium or an open one.

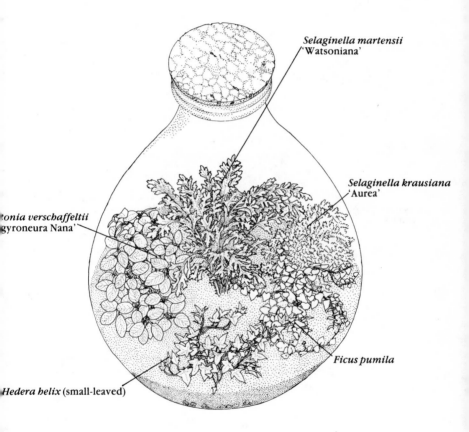

Selaginella martensii
'Watsoniana'

Selaginella krausiana
'Aurea'

*onia verschaffeltii
gyroneura Nana'

Ficus pumila

Hedera helix (small-leaved)

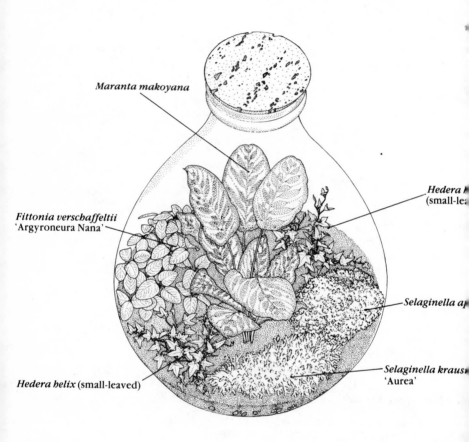

Maranta makoyana

Hedera h
(small-lea

Fittonia verschaffeltii
'Argyroneura Nana'

Selaginella a

Selaginella kraus
'Aurea'

Hedera helix (small-leaved)

PLAN 3
Bottle size: large
Type: sealed

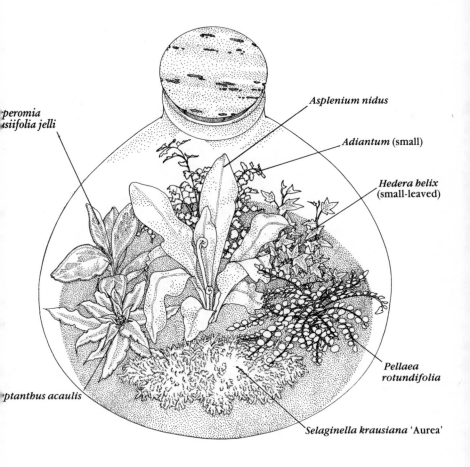

peromia
siifolia jelli

ptanthus acaulis

Asplenium nidus

Adiantum (small)

Hedera helix
(small-leaved)

Pellaea
rotundifolia

Selaginella krausiana 'Aurea'

PLAN 4
Bottle size: small
Type: open (preferably clear glass)

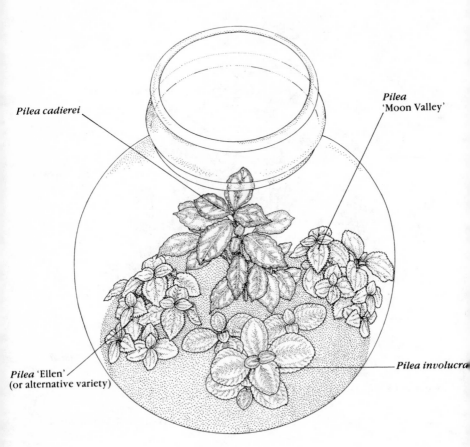

Pilea cadierei

Pilea 'Moon Valley'

Pilea 'Ellen'
(or alternative variety)

Pilea involucra

PLAN 5
Bottle size: medium
Type: open

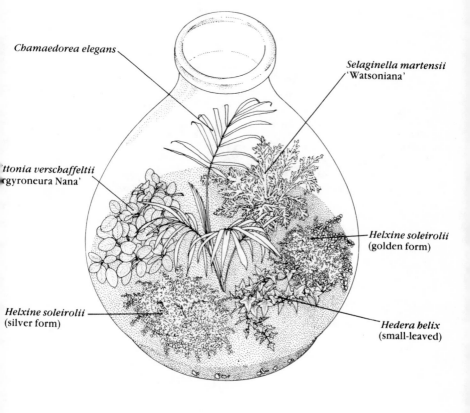

Chamaedorea elegans

Selaginella martensii 'Watsoniana'

...ttonia verschaffeltii '...gyroneura Nana'

Helxine soleirolii (golden form)

Helxine soleirolii (silver form)

Hedera helix (small-leaved)

PLAN 6
Bottle size: medium
Type: open (preferably clear glass)

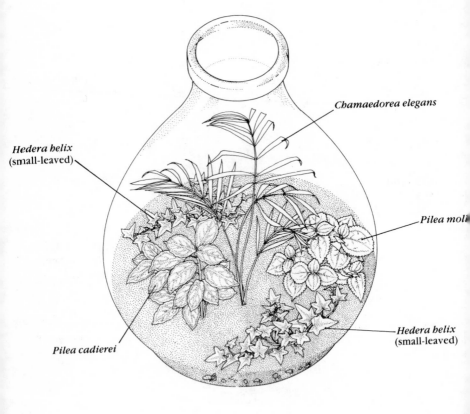

Chamaedorea elegans

Hedera helix
(small-leaved)

Pilea moll

Pilea cadierei

Hedera helix
(small-leaved)

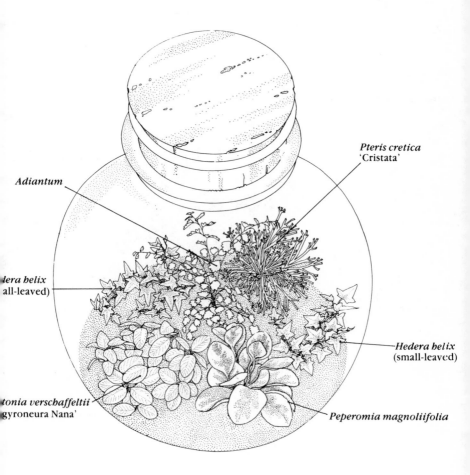

Adiantum

Pteris cretica
'Cristata'

...dera helix
...all-leaved)

Hedera helix
(small-leaved)

...tonia verschaffeltii
...gyroneura Nana'

Peperomia magnoliifolia

PLAN 8
Bottle size: small
Type: open (preferably in good light)

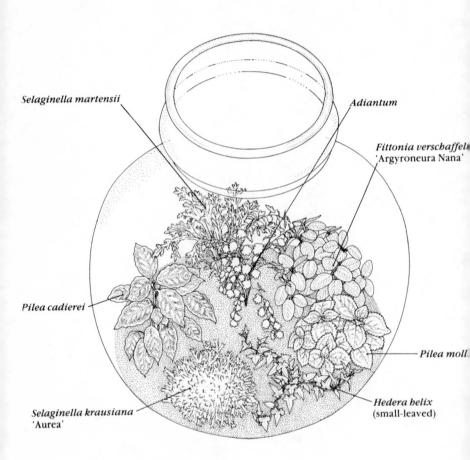

Selaginella martensii

Adiantum

Fittonia verschaffel
'Argyroneura Nana'

Pilea cadierei

Pilea moll

Selaginella krausiana
'Aurea'

Hedera helix
(small-leaved)

PLAN 9
Bottle size: large
Type: sealed (preferably clear glass)

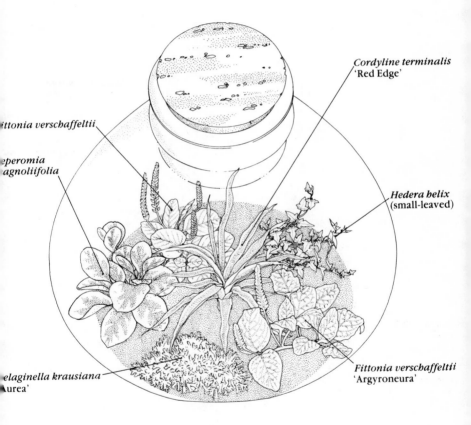

Cordyline terminalis
'Red Edge'

Fittonia verschaffeltii

*Peperomia
magnoliifolia*

Hedera helix
(small-leaved)

Selaginella krausiana
'Aurea'

Fittonia verschaffeltii
'Argyroneura'

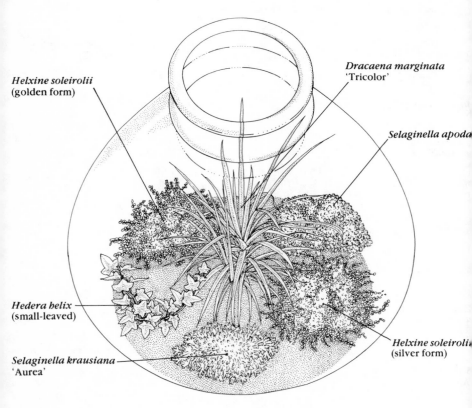

Helxine soleirolii
(golden form)

Dracaena marginata
'Tricolor'

Selaginella apoda

Hedera helix
(small-leaved)

Helxine soleirolii
(silver form)

Selaginella krausiana
'Aurea'

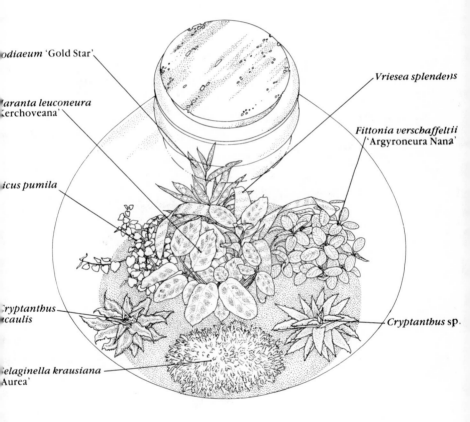

odiaeum 'Gold Star'

Maranta leuconeura
'Kerchoveana'

Ficus pumila

Cryptanthus
acaulis

Selaginella krausiana
'Aurea'

Vriesea splendens

Fittonia verschaffeltii
'Argyroneura Nana'

Cryptanthus sp.

75

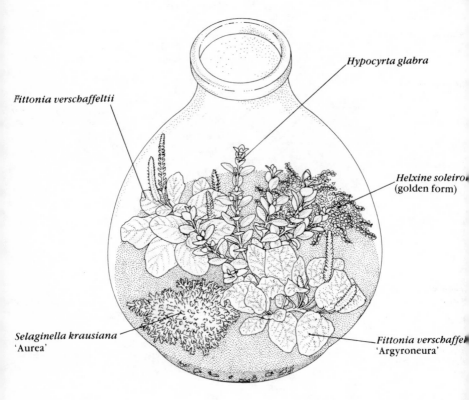

Fittonia verschaffeltii

Hypocyrta glabra

Helxine soleiro
(golden form)

Selaginella krausiana
'Aurea'

Fittonia verschaffe
'Argyroneura'

PLAN 13
Glass dome
Size: 25–30cm (9–12in) across and high

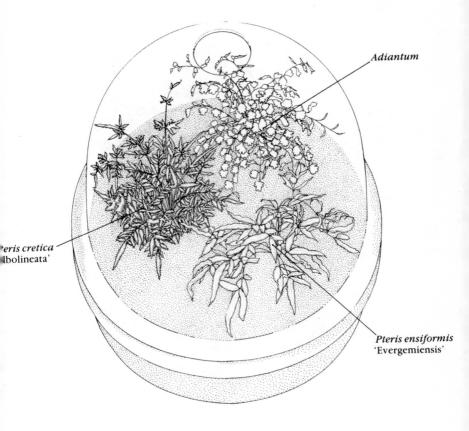

Adiantum

eris cretica
Ibolineata'

Pteris ensiformis
'Evergemiensis'

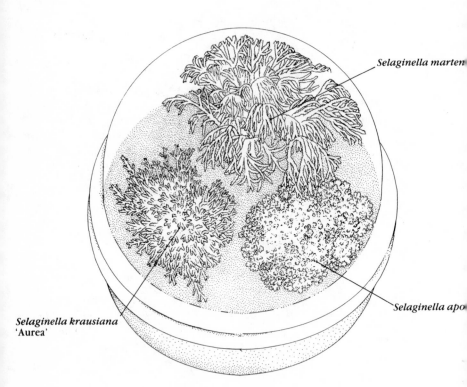

Selaginella marten

Selaginella apo

Selaginella krausiana
'Aurea'

PLAN 15
Aquarium
Type: sealed

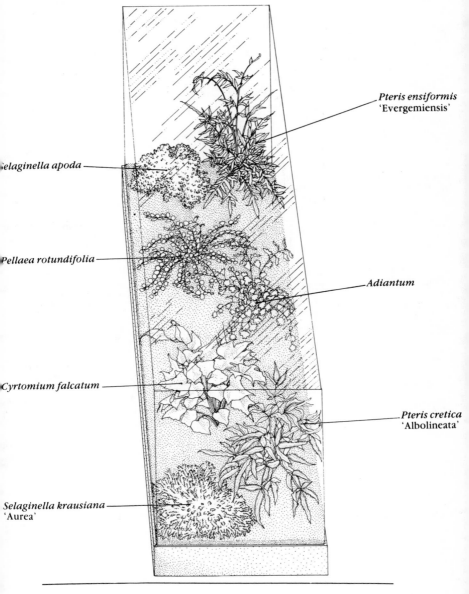

Pteris ensiformis
'Evergemiensis'

Selaginella apoda

Pellaea rotundifolia

Adiantum

Cyrtomium falcatum

Pteris cretica
'Albolineata'

Selaginella krausiana
'Aurea'

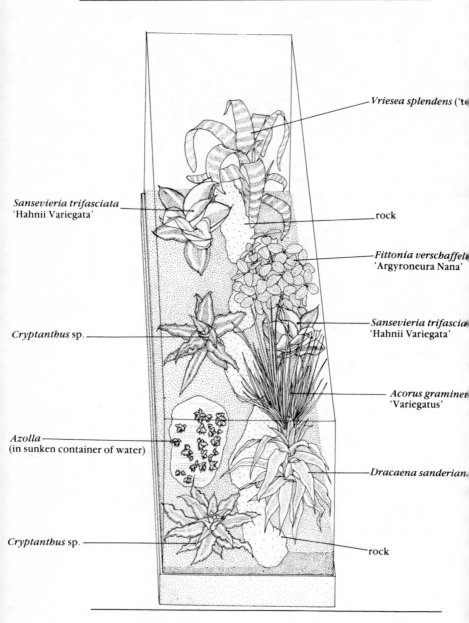

Vriesea splendens ('t⬤

Sansevieria trifasciata 'Hahnii Variegata'

rock

Fittonia verschaffel⬤ 'Argyroneura Nana'

Sansevieria trifascia⬤ 'Hahnii Variegata'

Cryptanthus sp.

Acorus gramine⬤ 'Variegatus'

Azolla (in sunken container of water)

Dracaena sanderian⬤

Cryptanthus sp.

rock

80

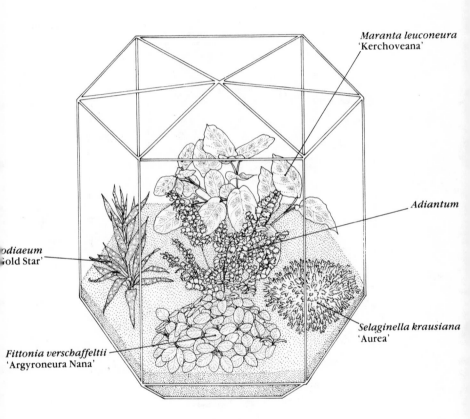

Maranta leuconeura
'Kerchoveana'

Adiantum

odiaeum
'Gold Star'

Selaginella krausiana
'Aurea'

Fittonia verschaffeltii
'Argyroneura Nana'

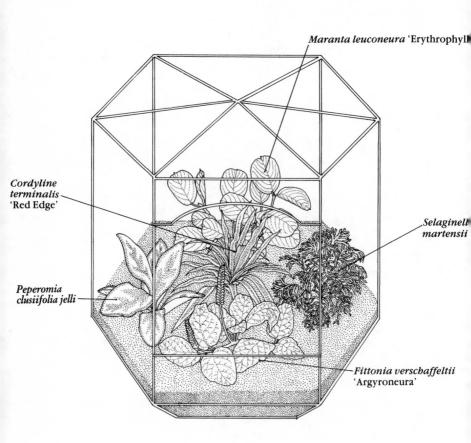

Maranta leuconeura 'Erythrophyll

*Cordyline
terminalis*
'Red Edge'

*Selaginell
martensii*

*Peperomia
clusiifolia jelli*

Fittonia verschaffeltii
'Argyroneura'

8. ROUTINE CARE

There should not be a lot to do to keep your bottle garden in good order once it has become established. There are, however, a few things that you should not do, and an even shorter list of things that you need to do.

FEEDING

Resist the temptation to feed your plants too often. It is better not to feed them at all than to overfeed them. You do not want them to grow too vigorously, and if they are a little starved they will remain small for longer (provided they are not drawn through poor light).

Most of the nutrients in a peat-based compost are likely to be depleted after a month or two; compost made to the John Innes formula may not need feeding for about three months even in ordinary pots.

You could use a slow-release fertiliser, which will provide nutrients over a period of about six months or so; but if you add these to John Innes compost you will probably be giving the plants far too much of a boost, and even peat-based composts will not really need them at first. They are particularly useful if you make your own compost, but this is not something to be recommended unless you can sterilise it properly.

A slow-release fertiliser can be particularly useful sprinkled onto the surface and lightly 'forked' in, about six months or a year after planting. Most of them release the nutrients only when the temperature is warm enough, so applying them in winter is not likely to cause a problem unless the central heating keeps the temperature up but the light is too poor to provide balanced growth.

Do not be tempted to use liquid fertilisers regularly, even in summer. In containers with no drainage holes, there is the danger of overwatering, and for the reasons already stated you do not want large, vigorous plants.

LIGHT

Plants need light, even ferns and other shade-lovers. Some need more than others, and the plants that can manage with least are often the ones that do best indoors.

The diagram below shows approximately how the light intensity is likely to fall in relation to a window. Obviously much depends on the size of the window, the aspect, and whether light comes from additional windows, but the broad principles apply. This diagram will be surprising if you are used to judging light intensity by eye alone; human sight can be very deceptive. Try measuring the light with a simple photographic light meter, then you will see just how much and how rapidly light can fall off within the room.

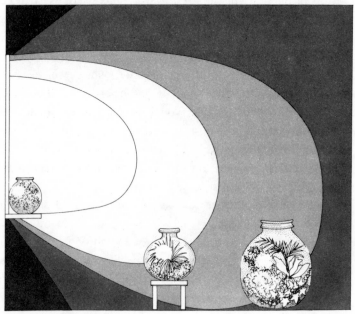

Diagram showing typical light fall-off within a room.

The green glass that many bottles for planting are made from can filter out about half of the light being received. So if you have it in a poor light position to start with, there will be a considerable shortfall for healthy growth.

Green-leaved plants will generally tolerate poorer conditions than coloured and richly variegated sorts, but even green plants will appreciate reasonable light.

The ideal place for a bottle garden or terrarium is in good light but out of direct sunshine. Direct sunshine intensified through the window and then the bottle or terrarium can cause excessive temperatures. The plants may be scorched; even if the glass is green the leaves could be burnt, because it is the temperature rather than the lack of shading that causes the damage (that is why well-ventilated plants in direct midsummer sunshine outdoors are seldom scorched).

WATERING

The trickiest job of all. With a sealed bottle it is difficult to get the water balance right initially (see p. 44), whereas with an unsealed container one has to strike a regular balance between over-watering and underwatering.

A moisture meter seems a tempting idea if you lack confidence in your ability to decide when to water, but there are pitfalls. After a time you will probably begin to find it a bit of a bore inserting the probe every time you think the compost might need water (though after a while you may begin to be able to judge this without the meter); more importantly you do not want to keep your compost as moist in an undrained container as it would be in a freshly watered pot, and the meter will not take account of the time of year. In winter, assuming that the light is poor or the temperature low, you should keep the compost in an open container drier than you would during the warm months.

You will find John Innes compost generally easier to judge than a peat-based compost, but both just need a little experience. If in doubt, keep on the dry side: if a plant wilts because it is too dry, water will usually revive it; a plant that has collapsed through overwatering is likely to be a write-off.

'PRUNING' AND SHAPING

With the exceptions of moss gardens or the right combinations of ferns, the chances are that some of your plants will grow more vigorously than others. So you will need to intervene sooner or later, both to keep the largest specimens within bounds and to keep a balance between the various plants.

Species that are likely to need frequent attention have been listed under plants for open containers in Chapter 6, but perhaps once or twice a year it may be necessary to open sealed containers to tidy the plants and maybe adjust moisture levels, and possibly to add a little fertiliser (but see cautionary note above).

If you notice leaves falling or stems starting to wither or rot, do not wait until the next 'routine' overhaul. Act immediately.

If access is no problem, use your hand to pick up or pinch off the offending part. This will be far easier, and probably more efficient, than messing about with special tools.

Sometimes you have no option but to do your surgery through a narrow opening. A razor blade firmly clamped in the split end of a narrow cane is usually adequate for cutting off leaves and stems. More difficult is the job of then removing the severed material.

A long spiked cane, or even a narrow steel knitting needle, may do the job if you are lucky. Otherwise you need to improvise a pair of tweezers on the lines of those described on p. 37.

As the plants grow you will probably find that they do not look quite as well placed and balanced as you expected when you planted six months or so before. If a particular plant has not worked well, do not be slow to remove it and substitute an alternative. This simple measure could avoid the need to replant the bottle.

Sometimes, moving a plant a few centimetres to one side may be all that is necessary. This can be done with the minimum disturbance to the rest of the planting if you scoop out a depression where the plant is to go, then loosen the plant and 'shuffle' it into place with the usual planting tools. Refirm the disturbed soil.

TEMPERATURE

The danger for bottle gardens comes more from overheating if exposed to fierce summer sunshine through a window than from winter cold in most modern homes.

Centrally heated homes present no problem; the dry atmosphere that spells trouble for so many plants will not cause problems in the humid atmosphere of a container garden. Even in an open container, the plants will do better than normal pot plants because there is usually a fair degree of atmospheric moisture within the container to provide a favourable micro-climate. The fact that plants are grouped together is also more favourable than isolated plants in individual pots.

In a closed environment, there is a temperature 'buffer' that means the plants are less likely to be damaged than exposed plants subject to widely fluctuating temperatures. At night, when the heating is probably low, the temperature within the bottle will cool more slowly than that outside.

Equally important, from the plant's point of view, all the containers described in this book are largely protected from draughts. It is often a chilling draught that is fatal for many tropical plants.

You must also bear in mind that all container gardens with mixed plants are a compromise. On the one hand they are likely to contain ivies that are really frost-hardy, and on the other they will probably contain plants such as fittonias and selaginellas from tropical rain forests. Although old books may describe many of these as 'stove' plants requiring a minimum winter temperature of say 15°C (60°F), they will survive significantly lower temperatures provided they are not overwatered, and not subjected to cold draughts.

As each home and each planting is different, the most sensible approach is to keep the bottle in a warm room if you can (but in a light place), and see how the plants cope. If you find one species does not survive well, remove it and replant with one that is more tolerant.

If the container is an open one, try covering it at night; a polystyrene tile may do the job adequately. If the bottle is by a window, you may be able to keep the plants warmer by placing large polystyrene tiles against the window panes. You will not be able to cover the whole window, but even if you can do it to a height a little above the container it should help. Books often suggest bringing your plants into the room at night, but a large bottle garden or terrarium is too heavy for most of us to want to lift twice a day. It is better to have it on a table or stand near the window but on the room side of the curtains.

During the summer, keep in a light place, but out of direct summer sunshine during the hottest part of the day.

PESTS AND OTHER PROBLEMS

Once a sealed bottle has been established, there should not be any pest problems, but open containers are vulnerable. Problems can occur even in the best arranged containers, of course. Unfortunately once diseases such as botrytis break out they thrive. The warm, humid conditions that suit the plants also suit most fungus diseases.

Unless you are sure that your plants are free of pests and diseases before you put them in your arrangement, treat them with an insecticide and fungicide.

Spraying plants in the home is always something of a problem. If it is summer you could stand them outside and spray with normal garden pesticides such as malathion and benomyl. In cold weather you cannot risk this, and then it is better to settle for some more suitable product.

There are aerosols for using in the home, though you should still avoid spraying them on furniture and furnishings. One based on pyrethrum and resmethrin will kill insect pests such as aphids (greenfly). Some insects, such as whitefly, are difficult to eradicate in one application, whatever the spray. If you can actually see insects on the plants, put them in quarantine after spraying, and repeat the treatment again after about ten days (follow the manufacturer's instructions).

A systemic insecticide, such as one based on dimethoate, can be watered into the compost to give protection for about several weeks. This also has the merit of being effective against pests such as mealy bugs and scale insects that can be difficult to control with contact sprays.

You can buy insecticidal 'sticks', containing butoxycarboxim, that work systemically. They are a convenient way of cleaning your plants up while in quarantine for a couple of weeks before planting.

Fungus diseases are always a problem to control once they have become established, and strict garden hygiene will do much to reduce the need for fungicides. Always remove dead and dying foliage and flowers as soon as you notice them — completely, so that stumps are not left to rot.

Two widely-used fungicides that are useful against a broad range of diseases, including botrytis (one of the most likely problems), are benomyl and thiophanate-methyl. Both are systemic in action, which means you can water them on instead of spraying, which is useful indoors.

If you use sterilised compost for your bottle garden, and clean, healthy plants, there should be no need to water the compost with a fungicide. It is sometimes recommended, but getting the moisture balance right is difficult enough without complicating matters. For the same reason it is not a good idea to spray inside a closed bottle. If you have pest or disease problems within, start again. Spraying inside open bottles should not cause the same problems, as excess moisture can evaporate.

Always check the instructions carefully before you use a pesticide. Some chemicals may harm certain plants (malathion should not be used on ferns or pileas for example).

9. NEW PLANTS FOR OLD

With luck, your plants will not die, but they may exhaust themselves or become drawn and straggly because of the poor light, or simply outgrow the container. So it pays to propagate a fresh supply of plants to take over when the old ones need replacing ... or to plant new bottles or terrariums as your enthusiasm grows. Even if you do not have room for more planted containers yourself, they make super presents. They look good and because you have planted them yourself they have that personal touch that is lacking in many commercial products.

For all these reasons it is worth propagating those plants that you can manage in the home. There are a few, such as codiaeums and parlour palms, that really call for better facilities than you are likely to have in the home, but these have been indicated under the relevant plants in Chapter 6.

If you have a greenhouse, and especially if you have a heated propagator, many cuttings will root more readily and more successfully than you can expect to achieve in the home. Generally, however, you only need a couple of extra plants, so even if only half as many root under the poorer conditions in the home, you will almost certainly have enough for your needs. Some plants can be divided, so you have new plants instantly.

The methods described in this chapter assume no special equipment, and nowhere better than a windowledge to root your cuttings or sow your seeds.

STEM CUTTINGS

Although the shape and size of the shoots may vary with the plant, the principle is the same for all of them. With the large plants the cuttings are usually about 8-15cm (3-6in) long, but with small bottle garden plants many are bound to be smaller. Even tiny cuttings will root successfully.

Cut across the stem with a razor blade or very sharp knife, just below a node (where a leaf arises from the stem). Try not to leave a long stump that may rot.

Trim the bottom leaves off, so that the part that will be inserted into the compost will be clear. Dip the end of the cutting into a hormone rooting power and shake off the surplus; do not be misled into thinking that more powder will mean quicker rooting. If you are able to buy hormones for different types of cuttings, one intended for softwood cuttings should be chosen. Some are intended for cuttings of all types. Many plants will root satisfactorily without the aid of hormones, but as they are relatively inexpensive and a container will do so many plants, it is worth using them as a routine.

Insert the cuttings into a 12cm (5in) pot. You could, of course, use a seed tray instead, but the chances are that you will only want a few cuttings at a time. Even if you are only taking one or two cuttings, it is probably still worth using a 12cm pot because a small pot tends to dry out more quickly and there is less of a 'buffer' within the compost.

Always use sterilised compost. There is a lot to be said for vermiculite or perlite for rooting your cuttings, but John Innes seed compost, or a peat-based compost, are all suitable. A mixture of half and half John Innes and a peat-based compost may give you the best of both worlds if you happen to have both to hand, but it is hardly worth buying the two specially for just a few cuttings.

Water the compost thoroughly once the cuttings have been inserted, then let the surplus drain.

If you have a small propagator, place the pot of cuttings in that. Even if it is unheated it should maintain a more even temperature and above all provide the necessary humidity. Failing that, simply inflate a clear polythene bag and place it over the top of the pot, holding it round the neck of the pot with a rubber band. If it is a clay pot, and you are taking the cuttings in the summer, it may be worth enclosing the whole pot in the bag, sealing the top with a twist-tie, to reduce moisture loss through the pot. It is important that the polythene is not in contact with the leaves, so it may be necessary to use bent wires or pieces of split-cane to hold it off the cuttings.

As soon as the cuttings have formed a fair amount of root, pot them up into small pots of John Innes No 1 potting compost, or a peat-based potting compost.

Always keep the cuttings in a reasonably light position but out of direct sunlight while they are rooting. Avoid direct sunlight for a few days after potting up. Otherwise, make sure that the plants have enough light to avoid becoming drawn.

Cane cuttings are more specialised, and you will probably only want to use this method for dracaenas among the plants in this book.

Cut the stem into sections about 5-8cm (2-3in) long, ensuring that each piece has a node (where the old leaf arose). Half-bury the stem in the compost, laying it horizontally, with a leaf bud pointing upwards. Keep in a warm and humid atmosphere, like an ordinary stem cutting.

LEAF CUTTINGS

There are various types of leaf cuttings that you can take, but those listed in Chapter 6 that are propagated this way, such as *Peperomia caperata* and saintpaulias, are leaf petiole cuttings (in other words, leaf stalk), as opposed to methods where the leaf blade is cut into sections.

Carefully remove the whole leaf, including the leaf stalk, and insert into the compost so that the base of the blade sits on the compost. You will probably have to use something like a pencil to make a hole to take the stalk — if you try to push it into the compost without making a hole first, the stalk will probably be damaged.

AIR LAYERING

On a large, bushy plant you can air layer individual sideshoots, but for bottle plants they are hardly likely to be as large as this. It is, however, useful if the plant has become leggy; even though you only end up with one plant at least it will be compact and fully clothed again.

A few centimetres below the bottom leaves (assuming that the plant has become leggy), make an upward-sloping cut about half-way through the stem. Be careful not to slice through the plant. Brush or paint a rooting hormone into the wound, and use something like a wedge of moss or even a piece of matchstick to keep it open. Then pack damp sphagnum moss around the stem. If this is not available, you can use moist peat instead.

Hold the moss in place with a sheet of polythene bound round the stem. Make sure there is a good seal above and below, otherwise the moss or peat might dry out. A plastic-coated wire twist-tie can be used. Black polythene is better because it encourages more rapid rooting, but you can use clear polythene if that is all you have available. Clear polythene has the advantage of enabling you to see when roots are forming, but you could have the best of both worlds by applying a second layer of black polythene (which you can remove to check on progress) over the clear piece.

Once roots have formed, sever the plant below the new roots, then pot up carefully.

DIVISION

This is by far the simplest method, and the most instant. Many ferns, marantas, and saintpaulias, are among the plants that can be divided.

Remove the parent plant carefully, and pull off one or two segments from around the edge of the crown. If the crown is very tough you could use a knife to separate the plant into pieces, but most can be pulled apart quite easily.

Pot up the divisions in small pots if you are not using them immediately, although you can put them straight into the new or replanted bottle or terrarium.

OFFSETS

Offsets are miniature plants produced around the main stem of the parent, though unlike a division an offset is not likely to have its own roots.

Simply remove the offset, using a knife if necessary, and pot it up. Let the offset root and become established before planting it in your container garden.

INDEX

Figures in Bold refer to colour plates, and those in italics to page numbers of illustrations. Captions to illustrations do not give Latin synonyms or common names; look up the main plant entry for the Latin name used - illustrations will be found in the index under that name.

95